GRILLING
FOR ALL SEASONS

BY RICK BROWNE

SELLERS
PUBLISHING

Dedication

This book is dedicated to my dear friend and barbecue godmother Carolyn Wells.
Carolyn was the person who first opened my eyes to "real" barbecue and the magic of barbecue
associations, contests, and festivals around the U.S. She has been an advisor, contributor,
consultant, and invaluable source of information about everything related to barbecue. I would
not be where I am today in the barbecue world without her guidance and help.
A big thankQUE goes out to a wonderful lady.

Published by Sellers Publishing, Inc.

Text and photographs copyright © 2009 Rick Browne
All rights reserved.
Front cover food photographs © 2009 Rick Browne
Front cover author photo © 2009 Kate Browne
Edited by Megan Hiller
Cover and interior design by George Corsillo/Design Monsters

Sellers Publishing, Inc.
161 John Roberts Road, South Portland, Maine 04106
For ordering information:
(800) 625-3386 toll free
Visit our Web site: www.sellerspublishing.com • E-mail: rsp@rsvp.com

ISBN: 13: 978-1-4162-0782-5

Library of Congress Control Number: 2009923847

10 9 8 7 6 5 4 3 2 1

Printed and bound in China.

Contents

GRILLING FOR ALL SEASONS
SPRING-SUMMER-FALL-WINTER BARBECUE

Yup, ALL seasons. Spring and summer and fall and winter. You can, and should, enjoy the pleasures and delicious tastes of barbecued and grilled foods equally as well amid the drizzles and flowers of April and May and the long steamy days of July and August, as you do on a crisp day in September or October while multicolored leaves fall, and yes, even in the deep snows and windswept, frigid afternoons of December and January.

In fact, in much of the country, folks who live in the so-called temperate climate states of Florida, Georgia, Louisiana, Alabama, New Mexico, Texas, Arizona, and California already fire up their barbecues year round. But why should they be the only ones to enjoy charcoal-grilled steaks, smoked brisket, and smoky pork ribs all year.

You know how much you enjoy succulent hunks of char-grilled protein, slathered with your favorite barbecue sauce, on a hot summer day. Well, you can get twice the satisfaction by serving up a slab o' pork, or drippingly moist beef brisket, or perfectly charred medium-rare ribeye on a gloomy and rainy November day, or snow- and ice-covered January day. Cold and rain don't really affect much when you think of it. If you've got a gas grill, no problem. And if you use charcoal or briquettes to cook with, all you need is a little more diligence in keeping the fire up to temperature.

Temperature is, after all, temperature. And if you've fired up your gas grill to 400°F on July 4th, you can be sure that you can fire it up to 400°F on December 25th. You merely brush off the snow, start the fire, put your food on the grill, close the lid, and retire to watch the game. And, if you are grilling a steak or something that needs more attention, you can just move the grill, as I do, to just outside of the doorway (a safe 3 feet) to your deck so you can stand inside and turn those t-bones over. Close the door to keep out the snow between turnings, of course.

December and January are two of my favorite months to grill, mainly because of the two big family-and-friends-getting-together-and-eating holidays they contain: Christmas and New Year's Day. But up to now, both have been relatively bbq-less.

Outdoor holiday cooking has two other distinct bonuses you may not have considered. When Aunt Mary and Uncle Mort; cousins Billy, Bobby, Betty, and Barbie; niece and nephew Frank and Fannie; your in-laws Ralph and Rachel; your own mother and dad, Wilbur and Wilhemina; and your best friends Paul and Paula come over for a holiday dinner, often the noise, confusion, and mix of personalities can be waaaayyyyy tooooooo much. Escape is as near as your friendly grill on the back deck. Just bundle up, grab a cold brew, and head for bbq sanctuary. Another good point about winter: The brew stays cold — no need for ice or one of those foam thingees when you winter que.

Plus, since piling all those folks into the house means you must cook enough food for the 10th Cavalry (you wouldn't believe how much Uncle Mort puts away; he ate half the turkey last year), you can easily run out of oven space in the kitchen.

Voila, a solution. Do the main course — turkey, roast beef, ham, etc. — on the grill, and, if it's a large enough grill, add a saucepan or two of side dishes as well, thereby freeing up the oven for the croissant rolls or cornbread, green-bean casserole, au gratin taters, pumpkin and pecan pies, and other vital holiday vittles.

To aid in your endeavors at breaking the bad habit of putting the barbecue away with the lawn mower, I've organized this book in seasonal chapters. In each chapter there are two suggested menus to give you an idea of a grilled meal, with breads, veggies, potato or rice, main courses, and desserts, all easy to cook up on your backyard barbecue. Plus, I've included lots of other recipes you can add in, trade out, or otherwise use as you wish.

But these recipes are NOT meant to be used ONLY in the season where they are featured. Yikes no! I suggest you try mixing and matching them: take a main course from the spring chapter, add veggies from the fall, throw in a bread dish from the summer, rice from the spring, and top off with a winter dessert. Or vice versa. Experiment, be creative, be confident and courageous. Here's an example of barbecue mixology: how about cookin' up Buttermilk-Chive-Cheese Biscuits (spring), Beer-Butt Chicken (summer), Harvest Skillet Corn (fall), Grilled Herbed Potato Slices (spring), and Pecan Pie (winter). Yum, I'll be right over.

As you choose recipes and menus to try, keep in mind that you can make almost all of these recipes in your oven or on your stovetop. I give temperatures for preparing the foods on the grill, but those same temperatures will work for oven preparation. However, as a master of barbecue, I hope you'll prepare all the recipes in this book on your grill (year round, of course). When you're melting butter for a crumb topping, or sautéing onions, you can just as easily use your grill's side burner as the stovetop — a perfect thing to do while you wait for your grill to reach the right temperature for the main-dish preparation. Conversely, try preparing your own favorite recipes on the grill. Have confidence cooking and baking outside and enjoy what has become America's most popular way to cook.

And, finally, for heaven's sake have fun with what you're cooking. Barbecue isn't rocket science, brain surgery, or even rocket surgery. It's a fun, safe, and delicious way to prepare food. But first, since we're setting out on the road to educate folks as to the wide breadth of barbecue possibilities, I'd like to share more than just the recipes and menu suggestions in each chapter. I'd like to share some guidelines, hints, techniques, tips, and shortcuts that I've learned on my travels to barbecue pits worldwide.

WHICH GRILL TO USE?

There are four main kinds of grills, and ALL of them will do a great job of cooking your barbecue meals. Most popular is gas, followed by grills that use charcoal briquettes, then whole logs or large pieces of wood (usually very large barbecue grills), and, finally, electric. Following the suggestions and guidelines that come with the units, you can grill, smoke, and cook both directly and indirectly on all of them.

BARBECUING VERSUS GRILLING

To me barbecuing and grilling are one and the same. This philosophy has caused me problems in certain parts of the country, like the Deep South, where "barbecue" means long, slow cooking times over low heat. To my mind, if you use a barbecue (the grill itself) to cook food on you're barbecuing, whether you're searing steaks on an open grill, cooking a pork shoulder at low temperatures, or smoking a whole salmon.

When I sear what I'm cooking over direct heat then move it to indirect (the unheated side of the grill), I often call it "barbecue baking," because it's so similar to when you "bake" in your kitchen oven. That term is unnecessary, but I feel it differentiates between "grilling" over high heat and "barbecuing" over low heat for longer times — all in the same device.

And as far as smoking: it's easy to smoke food on a barbecue grill, either by using charcoal or briquettes that contain wood chips, or by using smoker boxes or soaked wood chips in packets of aluminum foil which are then placed on or near the heat source to add flavorful smoke to what you are cooking.

And in all cases, whether barbecuing, grilling, or smoking, if your barbecue grill has a lid, close it! You wouldn't cook in your oven with an open door would you? (More on this later.)

BE DIRECT

Direct heating means just that. You are placing your steak, chicken, etc., directly over the heat source (coals, briquettes, gas flame, electric elements). We most often use it to sear the meat, and thus seal in the juices in the steak, roast, or poultry.

Grill set up:

1. Place all your charcoal briquettes, lump charcoal, or other fuel on one side of the bottom of a barbecue grill. Or, if using gas, only light half of the burners on your grill.

2. Place the food you want to "sear," or begin cooking, on the grill surface over the heat source.

3. After the meat or poultry has been over the heat for several minutes (time depending on what you are cooking and the recipe) and has grill marks, flip it over to "sear" the other side.

4. After both sides are seared (and marked with grill marks) move the food to the unheated side of the grill to finish cooking (again the length of time depends on what you are cooking and the recipe you are using.) See Indirect grilling below.

5. Close the lid for the remainder of the cooking.

INDIRECT

Rather than just throwing a slab of meat (or chicken or fish) on the grill directly over hot coals or gas flames, you should make a regular practice of grilling over indirect heat for the best results, in terms of moistness, texture, and also their third brother: taste.

You actually use a combination of direct grilling and indirect grilling, moving the food away from the hottest part of the grill, cooking it more slowly, over a lower temperature, and thereby keeping it juicy, tender, and loaded with flavor.

Most successful pitmasters place their meat, poultry, or game right over the hot coals or gas flames (400°F to 500°F) for short periods of time to sear the meat, thus helping to keep in the juices. Then they move the food to an unheated side of the grill (over a water pan, I'll explain this later) to finish cooking. I don't recommend this with fish, however, because it doesn't sear well!

If using charcoal, mound the briquettes or lump charcoal on one side of the bottom of the grill (leaving the other side empty for now) and start your fire as you normally would. Replace the grill rack and cook for high heat over the glowing coals first, then move the food to the unheated (indirect) side of the grill.

If using a three-burner gas grill, turn the outside burners on to a medium setting, but leave the center burner off. Two burners? Turn one to medium, one turned off. Gas is a bit harder to achieve low temperatures with so you may have to experiment a bit and use an oven/barbecue thermometer to check the heat. Try having the lid open an inch or two, opening the vents more, or opening the lid open all the way for 2 minutes every half-hour.

LIGHT MY FIRE

A barbecue "chimney" is important if you cook primarily with charcoal briquettes. It's a metal tube with a grate on the bottom. You load it with briquettes, place a crumpled two-page sheet of newspaper underneath the chimney, and light it with a match. Within 25–30 minutes the chimney has ignited all the briquettes and you are ready to use them to cook.

The other lighting aid that I suggest you use is an electric barbecue starter. It's basically a thick wire-heating element on a cord. You place it on the barbecue, cover the element with briquettes or lump charcoal, plug it in, and in a short time (15–20 minutes) the briquettes or lumps are ready to cook on.

It's important to preheat your barbecue, whether it's a charcoal, wood, gas, or even an electric grill. Most charcoal briquettes, if in a mound (without a chimney), need up to 45 minutes to heat to the right temperature, lump charcoal takes an average of 30 minutes, and raw wood logs take about 30 minutes to form the right kind of coals. And even instant-on gas and electric grills need time to reach full cooking temperature, so give these grills 15 minutes to fire up.

If you are cooking with charcoal or briquettes and it happens to be a cold or rainy season in your neck of the woods, you should have a second round of fuel ready to add midway through the cooking time. Cold air, rain, and snowflakes can reduce the temperature, thereby lengthening the cooking time. Don't add the second round of fuel unlit. Get it ready in a chimney or with an electric charcoal starter so you only add hot briquettes to your barbecue-in-progress.

SMOKING

To add a smoking element to the grill, take a 12x12-inch piece of heavy-duty aluminum foil (regular thickness works okay but I like the thicker variety) and fill it with a handful of wood chips you've soaked for 1–2 hours in warm water. Then fold over the foil to make an envelope. Prick 3 to 4 holes in the top of the foil only; do not go all the way through. Take this packet and put it directly on the coals or beside the gas flame under the food you are cooking. The wood will soon begin to smoke, flavoring the food nicely, and will last for about 20 minutes, the optimum time for smoking most meats.

Any flavorful fruitwood, pecan, oak, hickory, or alder works great and adds nice flavor. Do not use pine, as it contains oils and resins that can flame up, taste terrible, and make you sick.

KEEP A LID ON IT

If your barbecue grill has a lid, close it whenever cooking! You wouldn't cook in your oven without closing the oven door would you? Well, a barbecue is no more than an oven you cook with outdoors.

The only exceptions are foods like shrimp, thin fish fillets, or very thin steaks. When you will only be cooking 1–2 minutes per side, it's okay to keep the lid open.

However, all the rest of the food you cook should be seared first, with the lid open, then moved to the indirect (unheated) side of the grill with the lid closed. This keeps the heat and the moisture inside the barbecue, not floating into the atmosphere.

Be patient when barbecuing. Keep the lid on the barbecue closed. Every time you lift the barbecue lid you lose up to 15 minutes of cooking time. Get to know your barbecue, trust it, and limit your peeking time.

And if you are basting or spraying the food on the grill, do so fairly quickly to limit the time the heat is escaping into the air.

WATER, WATER EVERYWHERE

Just about every time I barbecue a roast, ribs, whole chickens and poultry, hams, or other large cuts of meat that I want to cook for a long time at low temperature, I use a water pan. The use of a water pan adds moisture to what you're cooking, stops grease splatters and flash fires, and helps keep the temperature inside the barbecue steady.

If you're using charcoal or briquettes choose a metal pan that fits under the grill surface. Place the water pan on the bottom of the barbecue next to the mound of briquettes or charcoal and fill it two-thirds full of plain water, and refill during cooking if the water is about to boil off.

If using a gas grill place the pan underneath the unheated section of the grill perched on the burners or ceramic grids that are heated.

You can add the zest of oily fruits (orange, lime, or lemon, for instance), or flavored oils (garlic, or hazelnut, or sesame), or vegetables with lots of oils (onions, garlic, shallots), to the water and there will be a small amount of flavor transferred. But it's a waste of time to add spices, herbs, chunks of apple, etc., to the liquid. The same goes for expensive wine, beer, or liquor. There will be no transfer of the flavor of the steam liquid. I know, I've tried with no success.

YES VIRGINIA, THERE IS A SANITATION CLAUSE

Clean your grills. Yeah, you Bubba, clean it every time. We've heard the old maxim: "that's a seasoned grill, all that caked-on stuff adds great flavor!" Baloney. To properly cook most foods, especially fish, the grill must be as clean as you can get it. You don't leave grease inside your oven or on your stovetop burners, do you? If so, I'm not coming to your house for dinner. That stuff is a bacterial theme park just waiting to "entertain" you.

To clean, wait until the grill rack has cooled down after cooking, then wipe off most of the grease and burned-on bits. If it's not clean, take the rack off the barbecue, spray it with an oven-cleaning spray, wrap it in newspapers, and put it back in the warm barbecue for 20 minutes. Then unwrap it, clean with soap and water on a sponge, rinse, dry, and you're ready to cook again.

Scrub everything you put food on or touch food with, in hot soapy water, and then use a capful of bleach per gallon of hot water to rinse. Wipe or air dry.

In regard to keeping food safe, allow food to come to room temperature before grilling, cover it, and don't let it sit unrefrigerated longer than 20–30 minutes. If you let it sit too long, you're inviting in Mr. Salmonella and Ms. Botulism for a long-lasting party. Keep all meats, fish, poultry, and dairy below 40°F if uncooked.

Wear rubber or plastic gloves whenever applying rubs, cutting meat or poultry, or otherwise handling food. And after using cutting boards, knives, plates, spatulas, etc., clean them in the dishwasher, or soak them in a bucket of hot water to which you've added liquid bleach.

HANDY GEAR AND GADGETS TO USE

Use the right equipment! Don't use tiny kitchen tongs, table forks and spoons, and oven potholders when you barbecue. Use the proper tools for a safe and enjoyable barbecue. Here's what we use in the Browne household:

- Long tongs with rubber grips and clamshell jaws

- Long barbecue spatula

- Dripless, heat-resistant silicone basting brush with a shield that prevents dripping sauce from splashing on your hands

- Barbecue gloves or silicone barbecue potholders

- Good set of 8–10 stainless steel kabob skewers

- Top quality brass grill cleaning brush

- 17-inch meat turning hook

- Instant read digital thermometer

- Electronic thermometer with remote signal device

- Food injection syringe

- V-Rack for ribs and roasts

- Plastic squirt bottle

THERMOMETERS

Most barbecue grills today have a thermometer in the lid, which gives you a good indication of the temperature inside the grill. However, the lid is several inches, and as much as a foot, above the surface of the grill, so you're not getting the correct temperature on the surface where you are cooking.

To be certain of your cooking (grilling) temperature, buy an oven thermometer (remember my assertion that a barbecue is nothing more than an oven you cook with outdoors?), fire up the grill and wait 20 minutes or so (with the lid closed), and put it on the grill in various places to check the surface temperature. At the same time, look at the temperature registered on the outside thermometer in the lid. Make note of the difference, so that when it's 350°F (for example) on the outside thermometer, you'll know the correct corresponding temperature directly on the grilling surface. It will be hotter. Keep a chart handy for reference.

Speaking of a thermometer, if you don't have a meat thermometer (a cardinal sin in barbecuing, YOU MUST GET AND USE A GOOD THERMOMETER!), the old "burning hand trick" works quite well. Actually it's only a "burning" trick if you do it wrong, but that title sounds better than a "warm hand trick."

*Rare: Palm facing downward, 5 fingers outstretched. Touch the fleshy part of hand at the base of the U created by your thumb and index finger. It is soft and springy when fingers are outstretched. This should be the approximate feel of a rare steak when pressed.

*Medium: Make the O.K. sign with your index finger and thumb. The same fleshy part of your hand is firmer, yet still springy. This is what a steak feels like when cooked medium.

*Well Done: Make a fist. The same fleshy part of your hand is firm, with little give, similar to a well-done steak.

DISHES AND PANS

Any pan or skillet that you can use in your oven can be used in a barbecue grill. The best by far are cast iron cookware, or Dutch ovens, which are meant for oven use. I try and stay away from putting plastic-handled cookware into the barbecue and merely use those on the side burner, but if the manufacturer says it's safe you can probably use even those inside the barbecue. However, remember that some barbecue cooking takes place at upwards of 500˚F, and might just exceed the suggested temperatures for the handles of some cookware made for stovetop use.

Cookie sheets, muffin pans, pie pans, or other similar cooking pans generally follow that same rule: if you can use it in an oven, you can use it in the barbecue grill. I do stay away from glass cookware, however, as I'm not sure that they can withstand the same heat as the metal varieties.

OILS WELL THAT GRILLS WELL

Before you grill anything, and after having made sure the grill is clean, you should oil it either with a vegetable oil or one of the new grilling sprays that are available. You do not need to oil the grill if you'll be cooking in aluminum foil, or in a skillet or saucepan.

If you want to use oil (canola or olive oil are best), take a paper towel, wad it up, and then, using tongs, dip the paper towel into a small bowl of oil. Wipe the soaked towel thoroughly over the entire grill rack. You can do this either before lighting the coals or gas, or when the coals are ready to cook on. It's perfectly safe to do this as long as you don't linger in one spot so the towel catches fire, but a brief wipe with an oil-soaked towel poses no risk.

If you want to use a commercial grill spray you must spray the rack before you ignite the coals, gas, etc., or, if the fire is already started, remove the grill rack from the heat and spray it, then return it to the barbecue. If you spray over flames or hot coals you stand the risk of having a ball of flame leap up from the coals, painfully burning your face, eyebrows, eyelashes and any facial hair.

AHH, THERE'S THE RUB . . . AND OTHER WAYS TO FLAVOR THE FOOD

SEASONING WITH A RUB

We don't actually rub. We merely sprinkle and gently pat the rub on whatever meat, fish, or fowl we are cooking. But it would sound silly asking someone for his "sprinkle and pat" recipe.

Rubs are simply a mixture of spices, some more creative and tasty than others, that are used on meat, fish, poultry, and sometimes even veggies when one is grilling, smoking, or barbecuing.

A simple rub consists of salt and pepper with paprika thrown in for color. A complex rub may contain 12–15 spices. But I think anything containing more than 6 or 7 different herbs and spices is a bit too much. Individual flavors get lost in too many ingredients.

One clever way to add rub is to squirt prepared mustard all over the steak, roast, or fowl, massage that into the flesh, and then sprinkle your spicy powder all over the meat. The mustard acts as holding substance to ensure that the rub stays put and the acid in the mustard actually starts to tenderize the meat. After cooking, the food will not have a strong taste of mustard.

MARINATING

Marinating is an efficient and tasty way to add flavor, promote tenderness, and give a personal touch to an otherwise ordinary chicken, brisket, or other meat.

The primary purposes of marinating are to tenderize the meat and to add specific flavors. The tenderizing is done by using acids (citrus fruits or juices, tomatoes, mustards, vinegars, colas, wine, or beer) and the flavoring is done with the use of herbs, spices, oils, or vegetables. You should always have at least one acidic liquid, and 1–2 favorite herbs or spices in the marinade.

Dry marinating is the use of herbs, salts, peppers, and spices that are rubbed into the meat so that the flavors migrate into the meat, poultry, and fish tissues. No liquid is involved.

Injection is sort of marinating in a specific location. You use a kitchen syringe to inject flavored liquids into the middle of various muscles and then the muscles are massaged to distribute the injection liquid.

For heaven's sakes don't use marinade — direct from the marinade bag — as a basting sauce or, horror of horrors, as a sauce base. Marinades that have been used on raw poultry, fish, meat, or other protein carry bacteria that are on the surface of the meat you are cooking. You must, repeat MUST, boil any marinade you have used for at least 10 minutes before you can use it to baste cooking food, or as a base for a sauce you serve with the food.

Here's an idea: After the marinade has boiled, run it through a coffee filter to remove all solids. Then pour the marinade into a squirt bottle, add a tablespoon of your favorite liquor or liqueur, and spray it on the food you're cooking. This method provides great coverage, and the alcohol adds a nice touch.

BRINING

Brines are salted solutions used primarily to add moisture. As a side benefit, brining can reduce cooking times somewhat, and help tenderize poultry and meats. Food that is brined stays juicy and tender during grilling or smoking. Sugar, spices, and herbs are usually added to the brine to add more flavor, but the primary purpose is to have the salt solution help the tissues soak up more liquid.

I usually brine meats, turkeys, and chickens in a resealable plastic bag. Pour the brine into the bag over the poultry/meat and store in the refrigerator for anywhere from 1–24 hours. Turn over and shake three or four times during that time to make sure all parts are well-brined. Remove the meat and rinse it with cold water to remove any excess salt and then pat it dry with paper towels. Discard the brine.

And while you can inject marinades, DO NOT INJECT BRINES. Again, they are primarily used to add moisture to meat and poultry through the use of salty solutions, and you cannot rinse internal salt out of the muscle it's injected into.

Brining works extremely well with turkey and chicken, but can also be used for larger pork roasts and loins, hams, or beef roasts. Just make sure to rinse off the meat before cooking.

SAUCE

Do not apply sugar-based sauces until the last 10, or even better, 5-minutes of cooking. About 90% of all commercially bottled barbecue sauces, and most of the homemade ones, contain sugar, molasses, maple syrup, corn syrup, or tomato sauce. These sugar-based sauces burn or char very easily and much faster than the cooking time of whatever you are grilling. We have experienced the tragedy of a mordantly incinerated exterior chicken, with a bright pink and raw interior. A raw chicken meteorite is not a good thing.

Spring Recipes

Honey Roasted Duck

500°F
indirect grilling
water pan

Marinade:

½ cup passion fruit juice

½ cup apple juice

1 (5- to 6-pound) domestic duck

¼ cup fresh lemon juice

1 cup clover or orange honey, warmed

½ teaspoon fine sea salt

½ teaspoon freshly ground black pepper

2 teaspoons garlic powder

½ teaspoon ground nutmeg

½ teaspoon dried thyme

1 cup Gewürztraminer or other sweet, fruity white wine

The most popular duck in America is the Long Island duckling, which is the direct descendant of four ducks imported from China (yes, they were Peking ducks) way back in 1873.

Heat barbecue grill (or oven) to 500°F for grilling over indirect heat, with a water pan under the unheated side.

In a small bowl, mix the marinade. Using a kitchen syringe, inject half the marinade into the breasts and thighs of the duck in multiple locations. Pour the lemon juice over the duck, and then, using a pastry brush, generously spread the honey over the entire bird.

In a small bowl, mix the salt, pepper, garlic powder, nutmeg, and thyme. Use mixture to generously season the cavities and outside skin of the duck. (Do not stuff the duck.)

Place the seasoned duck on the heated side of the grill for 15 minutes, turning over once. Then place duck in a roasting pan and move to the unheated side of the grill, over the water pan, and cook for another 35–40 minutes with the grill lid closed. Baste occasionally with the accumulated juices from the bottom of the pan.

The duck is ready when temperature in the thigh reaches 165°F and the juices from the thermometer puncture run clear. Be careful not to overcook the duck or let the fat ignite. Remove duck from the pan, cover it with foil, and let rest for 10 minutes.

Add the white wine and the remaining marinade to the roasting pan and boil for 5 minutes, scraping up any browned bits. Pour into a sauceboat and serve with the duck.

THE MOUTHWATERING MAGIC OF FRESH LAMB

During the past two years, while my wife, Kate, and I traversed the globe in search of the world's best barbecue (for my book, The World's Best Barbecue), we found to our amazement that much of the world eats lamb — except the U.S., that is. Lamb has always been unpopular here. Americans much prefer to eat beef, pork, chicken, and turkey, and I'm not sure why.

Some say it's the "gamey taste" of lamb. Nonsense, there is NO gamey taste unless the meat is spoiled or improperly stored and cooked.

Others say it's because of tradition. But since this country is comprised of immigrants representing many cultures and the cuisines they bring with them, I find that hard to (sorry) swallow. Scots, Irish, Aussies, New Zealanders, Italians, Greeks, Portuguese, Brits, Chinese, Israelis, Arabs, to name a few of the world's citizens, all include lamb in their traditional cuisines. But not the U.S.

Moroccans delight in their lamb tagines, the British in shepherd's pie, Greeks in lamb stews and moussaka, while the Scots and Irish love their stews and barbecued shoulders, chops, and neck fillets.

Lately there may be a tiny glimmer at the end of the culinary tunnel as young chefs, who take it upon themselves to travel and sample the world's cuisines, are beginning to appreciate lamb and offering it up in their restaurants. But the numbers of those who enjoy a tasty plate of lamb are still very meager.

The average American eats less than 1 pound of lamb per year. Contrast that with a New Zealander (56.5 pounds), an Aussie (30 pounds), Saudis (27 pounds), Irish (20 pounds), and Bulgarians (15 pounds). Compared to other protein sources we have available, lambs must be pretty happy to be born and raised in America. We do, however, chow down on 87 pounds of chicken, 17 pounds of turkey, 66 pounds of beef, and 51 pounds of pork annually. But apparently Mary still has difficulty finding her little lamb.

Some say lamb is "not available" or "hard to find." Balderdash. Currently there are more than 70,000 lamb ranches in this country. People just aren't eating lamb as a regular part of their diet. No excuse.

Washington State, Colorado, California, and Texas are the biggest producers of lamb in the U.S., with most of the lamb they raise sent to Los Angeles, Detroit, Boston, New York, and Chicago, where there are large populations of folks from Europe and the Middle East.

So here are some tips that will hopefully get you interested in trying this wonderful, healthy, delicious meat:

When shopping for lamb, look for good marbling (white flecks of fat in the meat). Lamb meat should be fine-textured, firm, and pink to light red in color. There should be moderate amounts of white, firm fat. Avoid cuts that contain fat that looks crumbly, dry, brittle, or yellowish — all signs that indicate that the meat is not fresh.

One of the most popular cuts, especially for holiday dinners, is the rack of lamb, which is made up of the unsplit ribs 6 through 12. The rack is usually split to make two lamb rib roasts. For special occasions, many people have their butcher sew two rib roasts together to form the circular and elegant "crown roast."

Other popular cuts include succulent bone-in lamb chops. Since lamb is such a tender meat, it takes well to marinating, and is wonderful in stews, kebabs, and stir-fries.

As with most meats, fresh lamb should be stored in the refrigerator or freezer immediately after purchasing, refrigerating it at 40 degrees or below. Fresh lamb will keep 3 to 5 days in the refrigerator, while properly packaged lamb can be frozen for up to 5 months.

Rosemary and mint are popular seasonings used in cooking lamb, as are tarragon, cumin, savory, coriander, ginger, saffron, preserved lemons, soy sauce, honey, and mustard.

❁

Crown Roast of Lamb with Orange-Mint Sauce

> 375°F
> direct grilling

1 (3½- to 4-pound) full rack of lamb

¼ cup extra-virgin olive oil

1 tablespoon chopped fresh rosemary

1 tablespoon dried savory

1 teaspoon dried thyme

1 teaspoon sea salt

1 teaspoon freshly ground black pepper

3-4 garlic cloves, peeled, thinly sliced

Orange-Mint Sauce:

½ cup orange juice

½ cup strong red wine (pinot or cabernet)

¼ cup finely chopped fresh mint leaves

2 tablespoons sugar

1 tablespoon grated orange zest

Pinch of sea salt

2 tablespoons butter

1 teaspoon cornstarch

In a recent survey by the American Lamb Board, 35 percent of Americans reported that they have never eaten lamb. Not surprising when the average U.S. yearly consumption is a mere 1 pound per person. This dish is an elegant and impressive addition to any festive occasion, any time of year.

Heat barbecue grill (or oven) to 375°F for grilling over direct heat.

When you ask your butcher to prepare the rack (sewing two rib sections together and frenching the ribs), make sure he removes the chine bone.

Brush the rack with olive oil, then sprinkle with the rosemary, savory, and thyme. Season generously with salt and pepper. Using a sharp knife, make shallow cuts all over the roast and insert a slice of garlic into each cut. Place the lamb on a wire rack in a roasting pan (so the fat will drain off and provide the base for the sauce), and then set the pan into the barbecue. Close lid.

The lamb is done (this will be in about 20 minutes) when a thermometer inserted into the meaty part of the rib, not touching bone, reads 125°F (rare), 130°F (medium-rare), or 135°F (medium). DO NOT COOK TO A HIGHER DEGREE or I will come to your house and beat you about the head and shoulders with a shepherd's crook.

Remove the lamb from the wire rack, cover it tightly with foil, and let it rest for 20 minutes. Remove the wire rack from the roasting pan, and place the pan over the heated grill or on medium-high heat on a stovetop burner.

Add the orange juice, wine, mint, sugar, orange zest, and salt, and bring to a boil, scraping the browned bits off the bottom of the pan with a wooden spoon to deglaze it. Reduce the sauce by half over medium-high heat. When the sauce has been reduced, whisk in the butter until smooth. Mix the cornstarch with 1 tablespoon hot water, blending well, and add to the sauce to thicken. Pour the finished sauce into a sauceboat and set aside. Keep warm.

At the table, carve the roast into individual chops and serve with the sauce on the side.

Moroccan Lamb Ribs

This recipe was inspired by a visit and short stay at the Rhodes School of Cuisine at the incredible Dar Liqama villa in Marrakech, Morocco. It is perhaps the best recipe for lamb I have ever tasted. Keep in mind that the ribs in this recipe must marinate overnight before being grilled.

In a 1- to 1½-quart pan over medium heat, cook the onion and garlic in oil, stirring often, until the onions are soft but not brown, 6–8 minutes. Mix in oregano, cinnamon, nutmeg, cloves, cayenne, brown sugar, vinegar, ketchup, and wine. Bring to a boil on high heat, stirring often, and cook 2 minutes. Let cool. If made ahead, cover and refrigerate for up to 2 days.

Place the lamb ribs in a resealable plastic bag with the cooled marinade. Refrigerate overnight.

Heat barbecue grill (or oven) to 350°F for grilling over indirect heat, with a water pan under the unheated side.

Remove the ribs from marinade and wipe off any excess, reserving in a small saucepan what remains. Place the ribs on the grill 4–6 inches above a solid bed of medium-hot coals or medium gas flame, cooking until the ribs are browned on both sides. Watch carefully, since the meat can be fatty and can quickly char.

After 8 minutes (4 minutes per side), move the ribs to indirect heat over the water pan and cook for another 12–15 minutes total for medium-rare.

While ribs are cooking, boil the reserved marinade for 12 minutes. Serve ribs with warmed sauce on the side.

350°F
indirect grilling
water pan
marinate overnight

Marinade:
½ cup finely minced onion
1 clove garlic, minced
1 tablespoon olive oil
¼ teaspoon dried oregano
¼ teaspoon ground cinnamon
¼ teaspoon ground nutmeg
¼ teaspoon ground cloves
⅛ teaspoon cayenne pepper
1½ teaspoons firmly packed
    brown sugar
1 tablespoon balsamic
    vinegar
¼ cup ketchup
2 tablespoons dry red wine

3½ pounds lamb spareribs,
    fat trimmed

Tangy Grill-Roasted Prime Rib

SERVES 8-10

450°F
indirect grilling
water pan

Rub:

1 cup kosher or coarse sea salt

1 cup coarsely cracked black pepper

4 tablespoons freshly minced garlic

1 cup Tang breakfast drink powder

1 (12- to 15-pound) prime rib roast with bone-in, cap off

5 whole garlic cloves, sliced thinly

Sauce:

1 cup port wine

1 cup favorite smoky barbecue sauce

Freshly chopped parsley for garnish

Freshly chopped rosemary for garnish

Tang was originally used on NASA's Gemini space program to flavor water produced as a by-product by part of the life-support system. It was not invented, as myth avers, by astronauts. Today it's sold in more than 30 flavors, and we've found it adds a wonderful "orangeness" to a barbecue rub.

Heat barbecue grill (or oven) to 450°F for grilling over indirect heat, with water pan under unheated side.

In a small bowl, combine the salt, pepper, minced garlic, and Tang powder, then set aside.

With a sharp knife, cut shallow slits in the meat and insert slices of garlic in each slit.

Spray the roast with a nonstick grilling spray or brush with olive oil, then sprinkle generously with the rub, patting it onto the meat.

Place the roast directly on the heated side of the grill to sear the meat for 10 minutes per side. Then place roast in a roasting pan and move to the unheated side of the grill. Turn down gas to medium-high (300°F) or close vents to reduce tempature to about 275°F to 300°F. Cook for approximately 1½ hours, rotating meat several times during the cooking process.

After 1 hour, check the prime rib with a meat thermometer to determine doneness, and then every 20 minutes after that (you don't want to ruin what many consider the king of meat roasts). Remove the roast from the fire at 118°F for very rare, 122°F for rare, 126°F for medium-rare, 130°F for medium. Cooking prime rib longer is a mortal sin. Meat will rise approximately 10 degrees in temperature while it rests.

Remove roast from pan and allow it to rest, covered with aluminum foil, for 15–20 minutes before slicing.

While it's resting, pour the wine and barbecue sauce into the roasting pan, heat to boiling on the grill, side burner, or stovetop, then simmer and reduce by about a third. Pour the sauce into a sauceboat, sprinkle with parsley and rosemary, and serve beside the meat.

Ham in Cola

4–5 pounds bone-in ham, at
  room temperature

3 medium onions, peeled and
  cut into quarters

1 (2-liter) bottle of cola
  (do not use diet cola)

Glaze:

½ cup yellow mustard barbecue
  sauce

2 heaping tablespoons
  molasses

2 teaspoons mustard powder

½ teaspoon onion powder

2 tablespoons dark brown
  sugar

Handful of whole cloves

This is a great recipe to use up that flat cola left over from your last party, but make sure it's not a diet cola (which turns bitter when cooked). It's best to have the soft drink at room temperature. The acid in the cola is a great tenderizer.

Place the room-temperature ham in a large, deep pot, flesh-side down. Add the onions, and then pour in the cola. It should come at least halfway up the sides of the ham (if it doesn't, add more cola). Put pot with ham on a stovetop or barbecue side burner over high heat. Bring cola to a boil, then reduce to low, cover the top of the pot loosely (with lid or tent of foil), and simmer for about 2½ hours, turning the meat once or twice so all the ham is under the liquid at one time or another.

Heat barbecue grill (or oven) to 325°F for indirect heating.

Remove ham from pot with a long fork and let it cool on a platter or cutting board. Save the cooking liquid.

With a sharp knife, remove the hard outer skin, leaving a ¼-inch-thick layer of fat. Score the fat with a sharp knife in two diagonals to make diamond-shaped sections.

In a small bowl, combine all the glaze ingredients. Using a spatula, spread the glaze over the ham. Insert a whole clove in the middle of each section.

Place the prepared ham in a baking pan on its side and set in the barbecue. Close lid, and cook for approximately 15–20 minutes, or until the glaze is bubbling and getting darker.

Meanwhile, in a large saucepan on the grill, side burner, or stovetop, bring the cola cooking liquid to a boil, then heat on medium-low heat for about 20 minutes, until the liquid is reduced by half. Take out the onions, if you wish; I prefer the character they add to the sauce.

Let the ham rest for 10 minutes, covered, on a warm platter, then slice and serve with the cola sauce on the side.

Rainbow Trout with Apple Salsa

ainbow trout is the most commonly farmed trout in the U.S. and is my favorite for this dish. However, you can also use brown or brook trout with great success. Lake trout, however, has a much higher fat content and is not recommended here.

Mix all the salsa ingredients together in a glass bowl, and let rest for at least an hour.

Heat barbecue grill (or oven) to 425°F for grilling over indirect heat.

Clean and pat the whole trout dry. Brush with olive oil, then sprinkle with summer savory and garlic powder. Put butter pats inside the belly cavity and salt and pepper the whole fish liberally.

Set fish on a sheet of aluminum foil on grill rack, which has been oiled or sprayed with nonstick spray. Cook for 3–4 minutes or until the fish flakes easily, then using two spatulas (NOT tongs) gently turn fish over and grill for same amount of time on the second side.

Remove fish from grill. Cut down the back of fish with a very sharp knife and gently separate the halves, pulling backbone and rib bones away from the bottom layer. Divide each half in half.

Serve the trout fillets with fresh lemon quarters and melted butter, serving the salsa on the side for everyone to add themselves.

SERVES 4-6

425°F
indirect grilling

Apple salsa:

2 red apples, cored, peel left on, finely minced

¼ cup lime juice

1 fresh jalapeño pepper, seeded and finely minced

½ medium onion, finely minced

2 tablespoons coarsely chopped fresh cilantro

1 teaspoon peeled and finely minced fresh ginger

¼ teaspoon salt

1 (3-pound) rainbow trout, or other local fresh variety

Olive oil

1 teaspoon dried summer savory

1 teaspoon garlic powder

2 tablespoons butter, cut into 4-5 portions

Sea salt and lemon pepper

Fresh lemon quarters and melted butter for serving

Buffalo Rib Roast with Orange-Molasses Glaze

SERVES 6-8

425°F
indirect grilling
twine
water pan

1 (7- to 9-pound) buffalo rib
roast or top sirloin roast

Glaze:

2 tablespoons extra-virgin
olive oil

1¼ cups (1 medium) finely
minced red onion

3 tablespoons finely minced
garlic

1 tablespoon freshly ground
black pepper

½ cup balsamic vinegar

1¼ cups fresh orange juice

1 cup root beer
(A&W recommended)

1 tablespoon grated orange
zest

⅓ cup molasses

¼ cup yellow mustard seeds

1 tablespoon chile powder

Sauce:

1 cup dry red wine

2 cups beef stock

Salt and freshly ground
black pepper

Buffalo meat is extremely healthy; in fact, it has less fat than turkey and chicken (even with the skin removed), has a delicious beef-like taste, and contains a high proportion of iron and protein. Plus, unlike beef, there are no known human allergies to this meat. Keep in mind that this roast needs to sit from 2 hours to overnight before being grilled.

Carefully trim the roast and remove all but a thin layer of fat. Tie securely with twine and set aside on a rack in a roasting pan.

Heat oil in a saucepan on grill, side burner, or stovetop, and sauté the onion and garlic until just beginning to color. Add the pepper, vinegar, orange juice, root beer, orange zest, molasses, mustard seeds, and chile powder, and bring to a boil. Reduce heat and simmer for 8–10 minutes or until glaze is lightly thickened. Cool.

Generously paint the roast with glaze and allow it to sit at least 2 hours, covered, at room temperature, or refrigerate overnight (best option). Reserve the remaining glaze to baste the roast during cooking. Before roasting, bring the meat back to room temperature.

Heat barbecue grill (or oven) to 425°F for grilling over indirect heat, with a water pan under unheated side.

Place the roast directly on the grill over direct heat for 15 minutes, turning once, then move the roast to unheated side of the grill over a water pan, reduce gas heat to 375°F, or close vents to lower temperature to same degree if using charcoal. Cook until a meat thermometer registers 130°F. Keep grill covered while meat cooks. Baste roast occasionally with glaze.

Remove the roast from the pan and keep warm. Add wine and stock to roasting pan and bring to a boil, scraping up any brown bits. Reduce slightly and then strain if you wish (I prefer to leave it as is with brown bits of meat in the sauce for more character). Add salt and pepper if desired. Put sauce into a sauceboat and serve alongside the roast.

Dr. John's Cedar Plank Salmon

SERVES 4-6

450°F
direct grilling
cedar plank

Marinade:

1 tablespoon balsamic vinegar

1 tablespoon ground ginger

1 tablespoon granulated garlic

2 tablespoons brown sugar

2 tablespoons chopped green onions (green end only)

2½-pound fresh salmon fillet, boned, skin on

¼ cup extra-virgin olive oil

Coarse sea salt

Freshly ground black pepper

Garnish:

½–1 cup fresh raspberries

1 cup water

1 teaspoon balsamic vinegar

1 teaspoon sugar

This recipe is dedicated to my dear friend Dr. John Davis, a lifelong Washington State educator, a world-class light bulb collector, and my most avid fan, recipe tester, and barbecue dinner buddy. He couldn't cook a lick, but he loved my barbecued beans, ribs, and this salmon dish, which I made him for his birthday.

Soak a cedar plank that's made for plank cooking (usually about ¼-inch thick) for at least 3 hours in warm water. I place it in a large flat pan and weight it down with a large unopened can of soup or a bowl of water, so it's completely under water.

While the board is soaking, mix the marinade ingredients in a small bowl. Place the salmon in a large oblong glass pan, pour the marinade over it, and marinate for an hour, turning the fish over once or twice.

Heat barbecue grill (or oven) to 450°F for grilling over direct heat.

Remove the salmon from the marinade (reserving the marinade), let it drain, and set aside.

Pour the marinade into a small saucepan and heat to boiling. Boil for 12 minutes, then cool to use as a basting liquid.

Remove the plank from the water, pat dry, and brush the top surface with ¼ cup olive oil. Place the salmon fillet skin-side down on the oiled surface of the plank. Sprinkle with salt and pepper, then place the plank in the middle of the hot grill. Close the lid of the barbecue.

Have a squirt bottle filled with water handy, as sometimes the edges of the soaked plank start to burn. If so, just spray them down, close lid, and continue to cook. The plank will end up totally charred underneath and on the edges; this is fine. But if it catches completely on fire, you must dowse the flames.

Grill, covered, for 20 minutes, or until the fish is cooked and the center is still just a little rare. Some of the fat from the fish will turn white along the sides of the fillet. Lightly baste twice during the cooking period, trying to keep the lid open for a minimal amount of time as you do so.

While the fish is cooking, gently simmer the fresh raspberries in water, balsamic vinegar, and sugar in a small saucepan, for 5 minutes.

Remove the plank from the barbecue and place it, with the salmon still on it, on a large serving tray over hot pads on the table.

Drain the berries and then sprinkle them on top of the salmon at the table.

Dungeness Crab Cakes with Basil Mayonnaise

SERVES 4-6

450°F
direct grilling

Basil Mayonnaise:

1 cup loosely packed fresh basil leaves

1 cup mayonnaise

2 teaspoons yellow or Dijon mustard

2 teaspoons fresh lemon juice

Pinch of cayenne pepper

2 tablespoons extra-virgin olive oil

2 stalks celery, finely minced

⅔ cup finely chopped sweet onion

1 pound fresh Dungeness crabmeat (or local variety)

2⅔ cups dry breadcrumbs, fresh if possible

¼ cup chopped fresh chives

2 tablespoons chopped fresh parsley

½ cup mayonnaise

Salt and pepper to taste

6 tablespoons all-purpose flour

3 large eggs

Olive oil or nonstick cooking spray for frying

Paprika for garnish

ost people don't realize that Dungeness crab is named for a small fishing village on Washington's Olympic Peninsula. While plentiful all along the Pacific Coast, the crab is most celebrated and enjoyed in two cities: nearby Seattle and not-so-nearby San Francisco, on the world-famous Fisherman's Wharf. If you can, buy fresh crabs, which should be lively and have a hard shell. If you buy cooked crabs, make sure the legs are tight to the body, and there is no black discoloration where the legs join the body.

Heat barbecue grill to 450°F for grilling over direct heat.

To make the mayonnaise, finely chop the basil leaves and mix into 1 cup mayonnaise. Add mustard, lemon juice, and cayenne. Refrigerate.

Heat olive oil in large cast-iron skillet over the hottest side of the grill. Add celery and onion and sauté until tender. Remove from grill and cool to room temperature.

Pour the onion-celery sauté into a large bowl with the crabmeat. Add ⅔ cup breadcrumbs, chives, parsley, ½ cup mayonnaise, salt, and pepper, and mix well. Using ⅓ cup of the mixture, gently form a 2½-inch-round crab cake with your hands. Set it aside on a plate. Repeat with the rest of the mixture, forming a total of 12 crab cakes.

Place the flour in a small bowl. Whisk eggs in another bowl. Place the remaining 2 cups breadcrumbs in a third bowl. Dip each cake in flour, then eggs, then breadcrumbs, patting the crumbs on softly so they stick to the cakes.

Heat griddle or large cast-iron skillet on the grill and sprinkle with a few dribbles of olive oil or spray with nonstick spray. Add the crab cakes and cook about 2–3 minutes per side until they are golden, adding more oil as required.

Serve warm with the chilled basil mayonnaise, sprinkled with paprika.

Buttermilk-Chive-Cheese Biscuits

If you don't have buttermilk, you can make a substitute by adding 1 tablespoon of lemon juice or white vinegar to 1 cup milk and letting it stand for 5 minutes.

✿

Heat barbecue grill (or oven) to 425°F for grilling over indirect heat.

Grease a heavy-duty baking sheet with oil or vegetable spray.

In a small bowl, mix the flour, baking powder, salt, and onion powder until combined. Add the cheddar cheese and lightly stir. Rub the shortening into the mixture with your fingertips. Gradually add the buttermilk and chives while stirring the mixture until it forms a soft dough. Turn the dough onto a generously floured cutting board or pastry board.

Using a rolling pin, roll the dough until it's ½-inch thick, then use a biscuit cutter or small drinking glass to punch out biscuits. Place biscuits on greased baking sheet, not allowing them to touch. Lightly brush the top of each biscuit with egg-milk mixture. Bake in the covered grill over indirect heat for 10–15 minutes until just browned on top.

Serve warm with butter and either clover honey or fruit jam.

SERVES 4-6

425° F
indirect grilling

2 cups all-purpose unbleached flour

4 teaspoons baking powder

½ teaspoon salt

½ teaspoon onion powder

¼ cup shredded cheddar cheese

2 tablespoons shortening

¾ cup buttermilk

2 tablespoons finely chopped fresh chives

1 egg yolk mixed with 3 tablespoons milk

Butter and clover honey or fruit jam for serving

Grill-Toasted Avocado Bread

direct grilling
350°F

2 large ripe avocados, peeled
and pitted

1½ tablespoons finely
minced onion

2 tablespoons fresh lemon
juice

½ teaspoon garlic powder

Dash of salt and freshly
ground black pepper

½ teaspoon ground cumin

1 loaf of French or Italian
bread

¼ cup extra-virgin olive oil

Paprika for garnish

Not many people know that avocados are really a fruit, not a vegetable. While the most popular variety is the Hass, there is also the Fuerte variety, which has a thin, smooth skin.

Heat barbecue grill (or oven) to 350˚F for grilling over direct heat.

In a small bowl or a food processor, mix the avocado with the onion, lemon juice, garlic powder, salt, pepper, and cumin. Stir or pulse until smooth (there will be a few small lumps due to the onion). Avocado spread may be made ahead, but do keep it chilled and tightly covered with plastic wrap.

Cut bread diagonally into ½-inch-thick slices and generously brush both sides of each slice with the olive oil. Grill the bread in batches over briquettes or medium gas flame, turning slices several times until toasted on both sides, about 3 minutes.

Serve warm slices of bread topped with dollops of avocado spread and sprinkled with paprika for color.

Grilled Bread and Tomato Salad

*Y*es, *I know this is a salad, not a bread, but its main ingredient is bread, so just sit back and enjoy. I actually had this dish in France and loved it, and heaven knows the French have great bread to work with.*

Heat barbecue grill (or oven) to 350°F for grilling over direct heat.

In a medium bowl, whisk together the garlic, vinegar, olive oil, pepper, salt, chives, cardamom, and basil. Set aside.

Cut bread into ½-inch-thick slices and generously brush both sides of each slice with the olive oil. Grill slices on the barbecue, turning often, until both sides are crisp and have grill marks. Remove the bread from the grill, cut into bite-size cubes, and mix with the garlic-vinegar dressing in a large bowl. Gently fold in the cherry tomatoes.

Sprinkle with parsley for garnish.

SERVES 4-6

350°F
direct heating

Dressing:

1 large garlic clove, minced

⅓ cup balsamic vinegar

¼ cup extra-virgin olive oil

¼ teaspoon freshly ground black pepper

¼ teaspoon flaked sea salt

2 tablespoons chopped fresh chives

Pinch of ground cardamom

⅓ cup finely chopped fresh basil

1 half loaf of French or Italian bread

¼ cup extra-virgin olive oil

3 cups halved cherry tomatoes

Chopped fresh parsley for garnish

Grilled Herbed Potato Slices

SERVES 4-6

350°F
direct grilling

Dip:

½ cup sour cream

1 tablespoon freshly minced garlic

1 tablespoon fresh lemon juice

Pinch of salt

Potatoes:

3 medium Yukon gold potatoes, scrubbed, skin on

2 tablespoons extra-virgin olive oil

2 tablespoons butter

1 teaspoon dried parsley

1 teaspoon dried rosemary

1 teaspoon dried oregano

1 teaspoon dried thyme

⅛ teaspoon cayenne pepper

2 teaspoons minced fresh garlic

Salt and freshly ground black pepper to taste

If you live in Italy, where there is no sour cream, or you don't have it handy, you can make a pretty good substitute by using plain yogurt to which you've added 1 tablespoon lemon juice. Stir well.

Heat barbecue grill (or oven) to 350°F for grilling over direct heat.

In a small bowl, mix the sour cream, garlic, lemon juice, and salt. Refrigerate.

In a medium saucepan of boiling water on side burner or stovetop, parboil the potatoes for 5 minutes, then drain and cool.

Cut the potatoes into ½-inch-thick slices lengthwise, leaving the skins on.

Heat the olive oil and butter in a cast-iron skillet on the grill. Add the parsley, rosemary, oregano, and thyme and fry for a minute. Add the cayenne and the minced garlic and fry another minute. Add the potato slices, then generously salt and pepper them. Toss the slices in the spice mixture to coat both sides, then remove them from the skillet and transfer directly onto the grill rack, which you've oiled well.

Grill potatoes for 10–12 minutes total, turning them over after 6 minutes to brown both sides.

Remove potatoes from the grill and keep warm until ready to serve with dollops of the garlic sour cream dip.

Apple and Sweet Potato Bake

Mace is a red web-like covering of the nutmeg seed, which is used as a spice. It turns yellow when dried and has a pungent nutmeg-like (no surprise) flavor.

Heat barbecue grill (or oven) to 375°F for grilling over indirect heat.

Peel and quarter sweet potatoes and cover with water in a large saucepan. Bring to a boil, then reduce heat to medium and cook until almost tender. Cool potatoes and cut in ½-inch-thick slices, then cut each slice in half. Cut apple slices in half as well, and sprinkle both sides with lemon juice to prevent them from turning brown.

Mix brown sugar, salt, cinnamon, nutmeg, allspice, and mace in a small bowl and set aside.

Grease a cast-iron skillet or coat it with nonstick cooking spray.

Arrange half the sweet potatoes in the bottom of the skillet, then layer half of the apple slices over the sweet potatoes. Sprinkle half of the spice-sugar mixture over the apples and dot with half of the butter pats. Cover with the rest of the sweet potatoes, then the remaining apple slices. Add the remaining spice-sugar mixture and the remaining pats of butter.

Barbecue over indirect heat in the covered grill for 15–20 minutes, until the potatoes and apples are tender and the dish is bubbling and browned. Remove and keep warm until ready to serve.

SERVES 6-8

375°F
indirect grilling

6 sweet potatoes

1½ cups cored, sliced red apples, skin on

2 tablespoons lemon juice

½ cup brown sugar

½ teaspoon salt

½ teaspoon ground cinnamon

¼ teaspoon ground nutmeg

¼ teaspoon ground allspice

1 teaspoon ground mace

4 tablespoons (½ stick) butter, cut into pieces

Curried Lentil Rice Casserole

SERVES 4-6

350°F
direct grilling

½ cup lentils

½ cup brown rice

1 onion, chopped

2 shallots, minced

1 garlic clove, minced

2 tablespoons extra-virgin
olive oil

1 tablespoon butter

1 teaspoon curry powder

1 teaspoon powdered turmeric

2 cups chicken stock

1 tablespoon lime juice

¼ pound fresh spinach,
chopped

1 (14.5-ounce) can diced
tomatoes, including liquid

Curry powder is one of the most popular spice mixes. It usually contains turmeric, coriander, cardamom, black and red pepper, ginger, cumin, granulated onion, celery seeds, nutmeg, ground cloves, and cinnamon. Easier to just buy a bottle of the premixed powder, I say. To make a hot curry into a mild one, merely add coconut milk.

Heat barbecue grill (or oven) to 350°F for grilling over direct heat.

In a cast-iron Dutch oven over medium-high heat on barbecue grill, side burner, or stovetop, sauté the lentils, rice, onion, shallots, and garlic in the olive oil and butter until the onions become translucent, about 5 minutes.

Add the curry powder and turmeric, then the chicken stock and lime juice, and stir. Place the Dutch oven on the grill, uncovered, close the lid of the Dutch oven, and simmer until the rice is tender and almost all of the liquid has been absorbed (about 20 minutes).

Add the chopped spinach and diced tomatoes, and stir well. Cover and cook for an additional 5 minutes.

Remove the Dutch oven from the barbecue and allow the casserole to stand, covered, for about 5 minutes before serving.

Green Rice Casserole

*S*weetened, dried cranberries (sold by one manufacturer as Craisins) are a colorful addition to this hearty rich dish.

Heat barbecue grill (or oven) to 350°F for grilling over indirect heat.

In a heavy saucepan on the grill or side burner, cook rice in chicken stock until it's tender and has absorbed all the liquid, about 15–20 minutes. Set aside.

In a small skillet on grill, side burner, or stovetop, sauté the onions and garlic in butter until tender.

In a medium bowl, combine the cooked rice, sautéed onions and garlic, milk, cheese, parsley, cranberries, egg, salt, and pepper. Stir until mixed. Spray a 1½-quart oven-safe casserole dish or Dutch oven with nonstick cooking spray and then spoon the rice mixture into the dish. Bake for 20–25 minutes. Keep warm until ready to serve.

SERVES 4-6

350°F
indirect grilling

2 cups uncooked white rice

4 cups chicken stock

3 green onions, white and green parts, chopped

1 garlic clove, minced

3 tablespoons butter

2 cups whole milk

1 (8-ounce) package shredded Monterey Jack cheese

1 cup chopped fresh parsley, loosely packed

¼ cup chopped sweetened, dried cranberries

1 egg, beaten

¼ teaspoon sea salt

⅛ teaspoon freshly ground black pepper

GRILLING VEGGIES & FRUIT

*B*arbecue. *Real honest-to-goodness red-blooded barbecue means thick juicy steaks, tender flavorful racks of pork ribs, and moist and succulent roasts, right? Well yes, but as your mother once told you, and I'm sure everyone's mother shared this kitchen wisdom...you have to eat your veggies, too! And since you love the flavor of barbecue, why don't you grill vegetables as well?*

Grilled or barbecued veggies are picking up in popularity as people discover that a bit of smoky flavor, some herbs and spices, and the right grilling techniques give even "old standard" vegetables a whole new taste.

Take a simple spud, brush it with olive oil or bacon fat, then roll it in a mixture of paprika, garlic granules, lemon pepper, oregano, and a pinch of cumin, smoke-bake it on your barbecue grill until the skin is crunchy and the inside is just fork-tender, and you've increased the flavor factor by about 259%.

Well, that same kind of approach to other vegetables can liven up your side dishes and will produce rave reviews from guests, and even family, at your next Que.

There's a whole new world of grilling out there that doesn't involve protein — either the bovine, porcine, or fowl kind. In fact, some folks, this author included, often find that a (OMG, do I dare say it?) "vegetarian meal" grilled on the barbecue is as satisfying as a hunk of steak, chicken breast, or slab of ribs (well pretty close, on the ribs anyway).

Think about the harvest bounty we have available in our markets: corn, snap peas, tomatoes, beets, parsnips, onions, potatoes, sweet potato, turnip, eggplant, acorn squash, spaghetti squash, Belgian endive, salsify, asparagus, cabbage, zucchini, cauliflower, Brussels sprouts, celery, artichokes, pumpkin, lettuce, broccoli, rutabaga, Swiss chard, bok choy, leeks, and green beans. And they are all delicious prepared on your backyard barbecue!

Some tips: First, before cooking, try to cut whatever you are grilling into equal-size pieces. If one piece of beet is small and the other large, one of them will be either overcooked and dry, the other undercooked and raw.

Peeleth not thy veggies! Leave the skins on potatoes, squash, eggplants, parsnips, carrots, etc., as the skin helps keep the vegetables in shape while cooking and also helps keep them moist. Just scrub them well before you cook. The skins can be removed after cooking, but remember the skin and ¼-inch underneath on many vegetables has the most minerals, vitamins, and phenolic compounds (which reportedly provide antioxidant and anti-inflammatory benefits).

For a new twist, try marinating the vegetables before cooking. Use a simple marinade (made up of two-thirds olive oil to one-third balsamic or tarragon vinegar, or fresh lemon or lime juice). Marinate for 1 or 2 hours, and then sprinkle in a few fresh herbs, chopped garlic, salt and pepper, and grill for a tasty side or even main dish.

Some more suggestions: If you are mixing hard (carrots, potatoes, etc.) and soft veggies (onions, tomatoes, squash, etc.) on a skewer for a kabob, think about parboiling the hard varieties to soften them up a bit so they'll cook at the same rate as the soft ones.

Along that line, you should almost never mix meat, poultry, or fish with fresh veggies on a barbecue skewer. Do them separately. It would take a "quelinary" genius to get them all to cook properly when they are mixed on a skewer.

Try not to cut any veggie slices more than ½-inch thick; otherwise, unless you are lucky, the inside will be uncooked and the outside will be charred. However, if you've parboiled the slices (potatoes, sweet potatoes, etc.) as described above, just place them on the grill and heat quickly to carmelize the sugars in them, and to add some nice color and barbecue flavor.

With Brussels sprouts, thick stalks of celery, asparagus, salsify, and broccoli, you should cut a 1- to 1½-inch deep "X" in the bottom of the stalks to help the tough veggies cook evenly.

When grilling onion slices, run two bamboo or metal skewers like a cross through all the layers of the onion from side to side, so the onion slice will stay together while grilling. Drizzle with olive oil or melted butter, sprinkle with a touch of balsamic vinegar and fresh herbs, and you have onion steaks. Yummy!

When preparing that salsify — a delightful, yet little-known and under-used vegetable — wash and clean the thick stalks under running water and wear rubber or plastic gloves while you do this. Otherwise your hands will become blackened as the ooze from the stalks is very icky-sticky. But the flavor of this seldom-seen and seldom-cooked root vegetable is incomparable — sort of a blend of asparagus, artichoke hearts, and (I'm not kidding) oysters.

And please, oh please, do not forget the abundance of fresh fruits. A profusion of oranges, peaches, melons, avocados (yes, it's a fruit), bananas, pears, and Delicious apples (and other varieties, too) provide us with a plethora of great dessert or side dish ingredients that are best, as with most veggies and fruits, cooked when they are in season. Grapes, however, like spaghetti, are better left off the grill.

Here's something new to try. Since avocados are a fruit, not a veggie, and are abundantly available in the late summer or fall, brush the flesh side with olive oil, grill just until grill marks appear, then grill on the skin side for 3–4 minutes, and then turn over and fill the hollow with fruit salsa. Now that's a dessert!

A simple syrup of brown sugar, butter, cinnamon, nutmeg, a pinch of ground cloves on a grilled slice of fresh pear or a juicy slice of grilled fresh-from-the-farmers'-market apple, and you've got a tasty, simple dessert. Or how about dipping pineapple slices into melted butter, followed by sprinkling them with brown sugar, and grilling them quickly over high heat. A dessert? Yes, but also a great side dish for chicken or fish.

Grilled fruit can be nutritious, not caloric (unless you put on too much of that syrup and brown sugar), healthy, and above all as tasty as the finest French dessert (well, maybe it's close; after all an éclair is an éclair).

The point to this essay is to remember that fresh fruits and vegetables should not be second-class citizens at any barbecue gathering. Properly prepared, cooked, and presented, they can share equal billing with the most mouthwatering slab of protein you can put on a plate.

✿

Asparagus with Lemon Marinade and 30-Second Béarnaise

*A*lthough I made this recipe using green asparagus, you can also use the white variety. It has the same taste as its green cousin, but because it's grown under the soil and never sees sunlight, it doesn't produce the chlorophyll that provides the green pigment. The white variety needs to be peeled completely and cooked longer until very tender.

Heat barbecue grill (or oven) to 350°F for grilling over direct heat.

Wash asparagus thoroughly and peel the bottom third of the stems with a hand peeler. Using a sharp knife, cut an "X" vertically from the bottom about a third of the way up each stalk. Put asparagus in a flat pan.

Whisk together the oil, butter, honey, pepper, salt, and lemon juice in a small bowl. Pour over the asparagus and marinate for 15 minutes, then drain and discard the marinade.

While the asparagus is marinating, bring the cider vinegar and tarragon to a boil in a small saucepan, simmer for 3 minutes, remove from heat, and allow to cool for 5 minutes

In a blender, combine the cooled tarragon-vinegar reduction, egg yolks, lemon juice, and cayenne pepper. Blend for 30 seconds while slowly adding the hot butter on high speed. If the sauce gets too thick, add a little water. Garnish the sauce with chopped parsley and set aside, cover, and keep warm.

Place asparagus crosswise on the well-oiled grill rack. Grill until lightly browned and tender, about 4 minutes, turning once with tongs. Transfer grilled asparagus to a heated serving platter and drizzle the warm Béarnaise sauce over the top. Serve at once.

SERVES 4-6

> 350°F
> direct grilling

1½ pounds fresh, bright green asparagus, with tightly closed tips
2 teaspoons olive oil
½ cup melted butter
2 tablespoons honey
¾ teaspoon freshly ground black pepper
Pinch of sea salt
Juice of 1 lemon

Béarnaise:
1 tablespoon cider vinegar
2 tablespoons chopped fresh tarragon
3 egg yolks
Juice of 1 lemon
Pinch cayenne pepper
1 cup butter, melted and kept hot
1 tablespoon chopped fresh parsley

Ratatouille on the Grill

350°F
direct grilling
2 bamboo skewers

1 eggplant, cut into ½-inch slices

2 large onions, quartered vertically

1 zucchini, cut in quarters lengthwise

1 summer squash, cut in quarters lengthwise

6 green onions, about 4 inches long, including green parts

5 tablespoons olive oil

1½ tablespoons balsamic vinegar

1 (14.5 ounce)can diced, peeled tomatoes, with liquid

¼ cup chopped fresh parsley

2 cloves garlic, minced

1 teaspoon dried savory

1 teaspoon dried oregano

½ teaspoon dried marjoram

¼ teaspoon sea salt

¼ teaspoon freshly ground black pepper

¼ cup freshly chopped basil

This wonderful side dish was prepared for me by Chef Patrick Payet at his home in Provence, France. The secret he shared: "Use only the freshest vegetables you buy that day in the market — not a supermarket, a farmers' market." He bought his veggies at the wonderful market in nearby Avignon.

Heat barbecue grill (or oven) to 350°F for grilling over direct heat.

Soak 2 bamboo skewers in water for at least 30 minutes. Wash the eggplant pieces and sprinkle with table salt; let sit for 30 minutes, then rinse and pat dry. Insert two bamboo skewers through each onion slice in a cross pattern to keep the onion slices from falling apart.

In a large bowl, toss the eggplant, zucchini, squash, and both kinds of onions in 4 tablespoons (¼ cup) olive oil and 1 tablespoon of the balsamic vinegar so each vegetable is coated.

Grill onions about 10–12 minutes over direct heat, turning about 3 times. Then grill eggplant, zucchini, squash, and green onions for 4–5 minutes total until they all get good grill marks on both sides. Green onions can probably be removed after 2–3 minutes so they do not wilt.

Remove vegetables from grill and cut into ½-inch pieces. Combine in a bowl and set aside. Keep warm.

In a large cast-iron skillet, sauté the garlic in the last tablespoon of olive oil, add tomatoes and juice, then stir in savory, oregano, marjoram, salt, and pepper. Heat on direct side of grill for 5–10 minutes. Then add fresh basil, sprinkle with the remaining ½ tablespoon of balsamic vinegar, and mix well. Pour the cooked herbs into the bowl of grilled vegetables and fold in.

Serve immediately from a heated bowl or platter.

Green Beans-Mushroom-Almond Sauté

*I*t's well known that mushrooms shrink during cooking. Here's a simple formula: One pound of large mushrooms yields approximately 5 to 6 cups of sliced mushrooms, which will produce 2 to 2½ cups of sautéed mushrooms.

Heat barbecue grill to 450°F for grilling over direct heat.

Place almonds on a baking sheet and roast in the barbecue for 5 minutes, or until they just begin to brown. Remove almonds and set aside.

In a saucepan over high heat on grill, side burner, or stovetop, boil 2 cups of water, add the green beans, and cook until the water evaporates, about 3–4 minutes. Set aside.

Melt the butter in a cast-iron skillet on heated grill. Add the mushrooms and sauté until soft, about 5 minutes, then season with lemon pepper and pinch of garlic salt.

Add the cooked green beans, and toss to coat. Sprinkle with toasted almonds and serve.

SERVES 4-6

450°F
direct grilling

¼ cup sliced almonds

1 pound fresh green beans, rinsed and trimmed

2 tablespoons butter

½ pound crimini mushrooms, sliced

2 teaspoons lemon pepper

Pinch of garlic salt

Barbecue Strawberry Kabobs with Balsamic Port Glaze

SERVES 4

350°F
direct heating
4 presoaked bamboo or
   metal skewers

Glaze:

½ cup balsamic vinegar

½ cup good-quality port
(such as Sandeman)

2½ tablespoons brown sugar

24 whole, large strawberries

2 tablespoons unsalted butter,
melted

4 ounces favorite blue cheese,
room temperature, cut in 4
wedges

6 biscotti (homemade or
store-bought)

F ar be it from me to dis a recipe, even my own, but you can get delicious results without making the glaze. Just sprinkle the berries with a sugar-cinnamon mixture (1 tablespoon sugar to ½ teaspoon cinnamon) and grill. But I have to admit the glaze does add a regal and finished touch.

In a small saucepan, combine vinegar, port, and brown sugar, and bring the mixture to a boil. Continue cooking until the liquid is reduced by half, about 20–30 minutes. The mixture should have the consistency of a glaze thick enough to coat the back of a spoon. Keep warm by setting the saucepan in a shallow bowl filled with very hot water.

Heat barbecue grill (or oven) to 350°F for grilling over direct heat.

Thread 6 strawberries lengthwise on each of 4 presoaked bamboo or metal skewers. Brush berries lightly on both sides with the melted butter.

Place kabobs in center of grill rack and grill until just beginning to brown, 1½–2 minutes. Turn skewers over and grill 1 minute more.

Lay each skewer on a dessert plate and drizzle with the glaze. Slice the cheese into 4 wedges and arrange on the plates along with a couple of biscotti.

Ken's Maker's Mark Cheesecake

By accident I once made this recipe without the sugar and found it less sweet but just as delicious. With a pound of caramels, chopped English toffee, sweetened condensed milk, and melted chocolate chips, this will satisfy most sweet tooths, but adding the sugar certainly doesn't hurt. Ask your dentist.

Spray the sides of a 9-inch pie plate with nonstick spray and dust with finely crushed graham cracker crumbs. Tap out excess. Mix the remaining crumbs with the melted butter and 2 tablespoons of the bourbon. Stir together, then press into the bottom and ¾-inch up the sides of the pan. Set aside.

Slowly, over low heat, heat the caramels and evaporated milk together, stirring frequently. When the mixture is completely melted, pour into the bottom of the pie pan, making sure it is covered evenly. Sprinkle the chopped English toffee over the caramel mixture.

Heat barbecue grill (or oven) to 350˚F for grilling over indirect heat, with a water pan under the unheated side of the grill.

Using an electric beater, mix the cream cheese, eggs, remaining 3 tablespoons bourbon, and sugar together until smooth. Add the can of sweetened condensed milk and mix well, then add the melted chocolate and blend completely. Carefully pour the liquid over the top of chopped toffee and drop the pie plate on the counter from 1-inch height to dislodge any bubbles.

Bake for 45 minutes on the unheated side of the grill, over water pan. Cheesecake is done when a toothpick or bamboo skewer is inserted into the center and comes out clean. Remove the cheesecake from the grill, let it come to room temperature, then pop it into the refrigerator to cool completely.

Serve with freshly made whipped cream.

SERVES 12-14

350°F
indirect grilling
water pan

1½ cups graham cracker crumbs

4 tablespoons (½ stick) butter, melted

5 tablespoons Maker's Mark bourbon

1 (14-ounce) package caramels

1 (5-ounce) can evaporated milk

1 cup coarsely chopped English toffee

3 (8-ounce) packages cream cheese, softened

3 large eggs

½ cup granulated sugar

1 (14-ounce) can sweetened condensed milk

½ cup milk (or dark) chocolate chips, melted

Freshly made whipped cream for topping

Chocolate Orange Shells

SERVES 4

500°F
direct grilling

2 large navel oranges

3 cups water

4 cups white sugar

1 cup boiling water

4 egg whites at room
temperature

1 teaspoon cream of tartar

½ cup confectioners' sugar

Chocolate ice cream (or
another favorite flavor)

Freshly grated or ground
nutmeg for garnish

Eggs that are at least 3 or 4 days old make the best meringue, and cold eggs separate more easily, but you must then bring the egg whites to room temperature as the colder ones don't whip as well. One more suggestion: Use 2 tablespoons of sugar per egg white, otherwise the foam won't last and the meringue will shrink.

Heat barbecue grill (or oven) to 500°F (or as hot as you can get) for grilling over direct heat.

Cover an 8x12-inch, ½-inch-thick wooden board with two layers of heavy-duty aluminum foil and set aside.

Cut the oranges in half, horizontally, and scrape out the pulp with a grapefruit spoon or melon baller. Place the shells, cut-side up, in a medium saucepan of simmering water on a side burner or stovetop. Cook for 5 minutes.

Using tongs, remove the orange shells, turn upside down in a strainer, and drain thoroughly.

In a large saucepan, mix 3 cups of the white sugar with 1 cup boiling water. On your grill's side burner or a stovetop, bring the sugar-water to a rolling boil, then turn the burner to low and add the orange halves. Simmer them for about 15 minutes, turning each half over several times to coat the insides and outsides with syrup. Using tongs, transfer the shells from the hot syrup to aluminum foil or waxed paper, cut-side down. Immediately sprinkle the outside skin with the remaining granulated sugar, then let the orange shells cool.

With a hand or tabletop mixer (mixing by hand takes way too long), whip the egg whites until they form stiff peaks, adding cream of tartar and confectioners' sugar slowly as you whip them.

Fill the 4 orange half-shells with large scoops of very hard-frozen ice cream, then completely cover the ice cream and top of the orange with a large dollop or two of meringue. Place the filled shells on the foil-covered board and set it in the center of the hot barbecue. Cook for 2–3 minutes, or until peaks of the meringue are just starting to brown. Remove from heat, sprinkle the meringue with nutmeg, and serve immediately.

Summer Recipes

MENU ONE:

Beer-Butt Chicken (58)
Grilled Garlic-Blue Bread (68)
Barbecue Fried Potatoes (71)
Tejano Corn Grill (76)
Rum and Coke Cake (77)

MENU TWO:

Ribs, Wonderful Ribs (54)
Buttermilk and Bacon Hush Puppies (67)
Rice on the Grill (72)
Que'd Bean Skillet (75)
Brudder's Sweet Potato Pie (79)

A LA CARTE SUMMER RECIPES:

Santa Maria Tri-Tip Roast (56)
Rod's Tequila Porterhouse
  Steaks (60)
PacRim Swordfish Steak (61)
Char-Grilled Lobster (62)
Pork Tenderloins with Spicy
  Marmalade Glaze (64)
Good Doggies! (65)
Kobe Blue Burgers (66)

Quadruple Cheese and Onion
  Potatoes (69)
Garlic, Herb, and Onion
  Potatoes (70)
Grilled Veggie Pitas (73)
Crisp Veggie Patties (74)
Grilled Cherry Cobbler (78)
Blueberry–Raspberry–
  Strawberry Lasagna (80)

Ribs, Wonderful Ribs

325°
indirect grilling
drip pan
wood chips

2 racks pork ribs

1 cup yellow mustard

Prepared barbecue sauce for serving

Brine:

½ cup packed brown sugar

3 tablespoons coarse salt

2 cups warm water

2 cups light beer (Corona recommended)

Juice of 1 lemon

Juice of 1 lime

3 tablespoons olive oil

First rub:

2 tablespoons dried summer savory

2 tablespoons granulated garlic

2 tablespoons paprika

¼ teaspoon ground cloves

½ cup brown sugar

Second rub:

¼ cup brown sugar

1 teaspoon cayenne pepper

1 teaspoon dry yellow mustard

This recipe calls for using flavorful wood chips to add a smoky tang to pork ribs. We suggest using fruitwood chips like apple, cherry, or peach, or mild woods like alder and pecan. All of these add a subtle smoke flavor without over-powering the meat.

The night before you plan to serve these ribs, place them in a 2-gallon resealable plastic bag. Mix the brine ingredients in a large bowl; stir well, and then pour into the bag. Seal well. Refrigerate overnight, turning the bag occasionally.

Drain the ribs, discarding the brine liquid. Pat the ribs dry, and then slather them with prepared yellow mustard, rubbing it into the flesh on both sides. Set aside.

In a medium bowl mix the first rub ingredients well and sprinkle racks of ribs generously with half of this rub mixture, set other half aside. Dry-marinate the coated ribs for 1 hour.

An hour before you plan to grill, soak a handful of wood chips in warm water.

When you are ready to begin cooking the ribs, place a drip pan in the center of the bottom of the grill. If using a charcoal grill, place the hot coals on either side of the drip pan. Pour 1 inch of water into the pan. If using a 3-burner gas grill, place drip pan over the middle burner, and turn the burners on both sides to medium. Fill pan with 1 inch of water. If using a 2-burner grill, ignite only one burner, place drip pan over unlit burner, and rotate the ribs 180° after about 1½ hours.

Preheat barbecue to 325°F for grilling over indirect heat over a drip pan.

Drain the presoaked wood chips and put them on a 12-inch square of heavy-duty aluminum foil. Fold the foil over the chips to make a small package, fold the edges twice to seal, and then punch 3 or 4 holes in the top (do not go through the bottom layer of foil) of the package. Place the package on one of the heated gas jets, or directly on the coals on one side of the bottom of the barbecue.

Place the ribs in the center of the rack, over the drip pan, membrane-side down. Cover the grill and cook the ribs for 2–3 hours, turning two or three times.

Combine the ingredients for the second rub; set aside.

When the ribs are tender, and the meat has shrunk back from the end of the bones by ¼-inch or so, transfer the ribs to a large double-layer sheet of heavy-duty aluminum foil. Sprinkle the second rub over the meat side of the ribs. Seal the ribs in the foil and place back on the grill for 20 minutes. Close grill.

Remove the ribs from the grill, cut them apart, and serve on a heated platter with a tangy barbecue sauce on the side, and accompanied by coleslaw, baked beans, and cornbread or corn muffins.

Santa Maria Tri-Tip Roast

SERVES 6-8

425°F
indirect grilling
marinate overnight
twine

1 large (4- to 5-pound) tri-tip beef roast (also known as bottom sirloin)

3 tablespoons minced garlic

1 large onion, minced

¼ cup melted clarified butter

¼ cup olive oil

¼ cup A-1 steak sauce

1 teaspoon Tabasco sauce

1 cup Chianti (or dry red wine)

Several long rosemary branches (to use as a basting brush)

Hoagie or sourdough rolls and garlic butter for serving

If you ever get the chance to go to Santa Maria, California, about 50 miles north of Santa Barbara on Highway 101, you must stop at the Santa Maria Inn and order their Traditional Santa Maria Tri-Tip, one of the best barbecued meats on the planet. My mouth waters just writing this....

Put tri-tip roast into a 1-gallon resealable plastic bag, add the garlic, onion, butter, oil, sauces, and wine, and seal the bag. Let roast marinate in the bag overnight in the refrigerator.

Heat barbecue grill (or oven) to 425°F for grilling over indirect heat.

Prepare wood or charcoal fire, piling coals or briquettes on one side of barbecue. If using gas, turn on one bank of burners.

Remove roast from bag with marinade and set aside. Pour the marinade into a saucepan, bring to a boil, and let boil for at least 10 minutes. Remove from heat and let cool.

Tie several long rosemary branches together at one end to form a basting brush. Let the brush stand in the cooling marinade.

Put meat on the unheated side of the barbecue. Cover barbecue and cook for 30–40 minutes. Use the rosemary brush to baste the meat with the marinade 3-4 times as it cooks. Use a meat thermometer to check the temperature of the roast. When the thermometer registers 135°F for rare or 155°F for medium, remove the roast from the grill.

Cover the finished roast with aluminum foil, and allow it to stand 15–20 minutes before carving — the meat will continue to rise in temperature to reach 140°F for rare and 160°F for medium.

While the roast is standing, slather rolls with garlic butter and toast them on the grill. Carve meat across the grain into thin slices and serve on the rolls.

You're Putting the Beer Can Where?

I first discovered the wonders of Beer-Butt Chicken quite by accident. Carolyn Wells, the president of the Kansas City Barbeque Society, was giving me a tour of the Blue Springs Barbeque Championships in Blue Springs, Kansas. As we rounded a corner and began walking past a whole line of kettle-type barbecues, a swarthy cowboy lifted the lid of his que and revealed the strangest thing I'd ever seen on a barbecue.

"What's that?" I asked, being the ever-curious journalist. "Why, ain't you ever seen beer-butt chicken?" he retorted. "That's the ONLY way to cook chicken!" Armed with this new knowledge, I approached his barbecue and took a closer look. Sure enough, a chicken was "sitting" on a beer can. Well, not actually sitting — the beer can had been inserted, as the common folks say, where the sun don't shine.

The cowboy chef explained that the beer flavors and moistens the inside of the bird while the heat from the charcoal cooks the outside. He explained this in a whisper, looking over his shoulder as if spies were watching his every move. "Sounds good to me," I said, "perhaps I'll try it."

Well several weeks later I tried it, and you know what it was? You guessed it — the best way I've ever had chicken, just as the cowpoke had predicted.

And since that time I've sorta become the "Godfather of beer-butt chicken," according to People *magazine, and I believe I was the first to ever publish a recipe for it in a cookbook.*

I was the first to demonstrate it on national TV in a July, 1999, appearance on Fox Friends morning show, live from Sixth Avenue in Manhattan. Then two months later I appeared on Regis & Kathie Lee. *Regis, I have to confess, held the chicken and beer can horizontally and gave his shoes a beer bath. But they enjoyed tasting the chicken I prepared.*

Then a Today Show *appearance had Al Roker grabbing off a wing and devouring it with relish after the cameras blinked off at the end of the show.*

Since then I've beer-butted hundreds of hapless birds in cooking demos, sponsor promotions, TV appearances, and newspaper photo shoots. It's become my "signature dish" and has drawn 100 percent rave reviews from anyone and everyone who has ever tried it.

Wow, all this because of an aluminum can shoved into the nether regions of a member of the poultry family on a small fairgrounds in the middle of Kansas.

Ain't America wonderful?

SERVES 4-6

> 375°F
> indirect grilling
> water pan
> spray bottle

Rub:
1 teaspoon brown sugar

1 teaspoon garlic powder

1 teaspoon onion powder

1 teaspoon dried summer savory

¼ teaspoon cayenne pepper

1 teaspoon chile powder

1 teaspoon paprika

1 teaspoon dry yellow mustard

1 tablespoon finely ground sea salt

1 (4- to 5-pound) whole chicken

1 (12-ounce) can of your favorite beer

1 cup apple cider

2 tablespoons olive oil

2 tablespoons balsamic vinegar

At one time I was the photo editor of a southern Washington State newspaper. When I was given a retirement party, one of the editors came up to me and said: "Remember, when you're rich, famous, and a TV star, that your success is based on the fact that you shove an aluminum can up the nether end of a dead chicken." Remembering that prevents any attack of ego.

Make the rub in a small bowl by combining all the ingredients, and stir until it's well mixed.

Wash and dry the chicken, then spray with nonstick spray or rub with olive oil. Sprinkle the rub all over the chicken, including the cavity. Work the mixture gently into the skin and under the skin wherever possible. Cover the chicken and set aside at room temperature for 30 minutes.

Pour half of the can of beer into a spray bottle, then add the cider, olive oil, and vinegar and set aside.

Preheat charcoal or gas barbecue for grilling over indirect heat over a water pan at 375°F.

Hold the half-full beer can in one hand and slide the chicken tail-side down over the can. This position and method does two things: first, it helps drain off fat as the chicken cooks; second, the beer steams the inside of the chicken, while the outside is cooked by the heat from the barbecue — making this method the moistest way to cook a chicken.

Place the chicken on the can on the hot part of the grill, cover, and cook for 20 minutes, spraying with the beer-cider basting spray once or twice during that time.

Move the chicken to indirect heat over a water pan (to keep chicken moist and prevent grease flare-ups), and cook for 1 to 1½ hours in a covered grill. Spray with the basting spray several times. The chicken is done when a meat thermometer inserted in the thigh reads 180°F. It will be brown, very brown; in fact, many times it reaches a mahogany color.

Remove the chicken from the barbecue and present it on-the-can to your guests. Remove the chicken from the beer can with tongs, while holding the can with a barbecue glove. Be careful as the can and liquid inside are very hot.

Give the chicken one more spritz of the basting spray and then carve and serve. Actually, by using rubber gloves, you can literally pull the chicken apart with your hands — it's that moist and tender.

Rod's Tequila Porterhouse Steak

SERVES 4-6

500°F
direct/indirect grilling

Marinade:

¼ cup soy sauce

½ cup extra-virgin olive oil

4 ounces good-quality tequila

1 (2-pound) choice porterhouse steak, aged

Rub:

1 garlic clove, crushed

2 tablespoons lime juice

2 tablespoons pineapple
juice

¼ cup butter, melted

Dash of balsamic vinegar

2 teaspoons lemon pepper

2 teaspoons seasoned salt

1 or 2 pats of butter

Rod was the best friend I ever had or will have. He was like a brother to me and the source of many moments of joy, laughter, and fun times. He loved my cooking and particularly loved this dish, which I cooked once at a barbecue at my home. He was a trucker and sadly passed away alone, on a back road in Montana, and I think of him every time I pass a semi trailer. But man oh man, he loved to eat, to laugh, to golf, and to do gentle, nice things for everyone he met.

Mix the soy sauce, olive oil, and 2 ounces of the tequila together in a large re-sealable plastic bag. Shake until well mixed. Add steak, seal bag, and marinate at room temperature for 1 hour.

Heat barbecue grill (or oven) to 500°F (or as close as you can get to that) for grilling over direct and indirect heat.

Mix all the ingredients for the rub in a large glass bowl. After draining the steak, apply the rub to both sides of the meat, rubbing it in with your hands. Let sit for 30 minutes.

Place the steak on the grill over the hot fire and cook for 2 minutes per side, then move steak to a cooler part of the grill, cover, and cook for approximately 3 minutes more per side for medium-rare.

Just before serving the steak, place the meat on a very hot platter, slip a pat of butter on top, cover with foil, and wait exactly 5 minutes. Then, drizzle the remaining 2 ounces of tequila over the steak and serve immediately.

PacRim Swordfish Steaks

Swordfish, one of the billfish, is usually available in steaks, loins, and fillets. Ask for Broadbill, Espada, or Emperador that are caught in U.S. Pacific waters with long lines, harpoons, or hand lines only. Avoid swordfish imported from international long line fleets because their fishing methods kill sea turtles, birds, and sharks in great numbers.

☀

Combine all the marinade ingredients in a food processor and pulse to combine into a smooth liquid. Rub the swordfish steaks with the marinade, place in resealable plastic bags, and marinate in the refrigerator for 1 hour.

Heat barbecue grill (or oven) to 375°F for grilling over direct heat.

Make the vinaigrette by mixing the vinegar and mustard in the bowl of the food processor. Pulse briefly, then add the herbs, pulsing until they are coarsely chopped. Add the olive oil very slowly while the processor is running, processing until the mixture emulsifies into a smooth blend. Season with salt and pepper to taste. Set aside.

Remove the swordfish from the marinade. Pat dry and let steaks come to room temperature for 10–15 minutes, covered. Grill the steaks on a covered grill until they have good grill marks on both sides and the interior of the steaks is cooked medium and is still moist, approximately 3–4 minutes per side.

Remove the swordfish steaks from the grill and arrange on a platter or serving plates. Drizzle with vinaigrette and serve with grilled vegetables and steamed fragrant rice.

SERVES 4-6

375°F
direct grilling

Marinade:

⅓ cup olive oil

Juice of 3 limes (or 2 large lemons)

1 jalapeño pepper, seeded

2 whole garlic cloves, peeled

¼ cup loosely packed fresh cilantro leaves

1 teaspoon freshly ground black pepper

¼ cup grated fresh ginger

½ cup unsweetened coconut milk

4 (¾-inch-thick, 7- to 8-ounce) swordfish steaks

Herb Vinaigrette:

¼ cup balsamic vinegar

1 tablespoon Dijon mustard

1 teaspoon fresh thyme leaves

1 teaspoon fresh oregano leaves

8 large fresh basil leaves

½ cup extra-virgin olive oil

Salt and freshly ground black pepper to taste

Char-Grilled Lobster

SERVES 4-6

> 400°F
> direct grilling

2 shallots, minced

4 cloves garlic, mashed

2 tablespoons olive oil

1 pound salted butter

¼ cup chopped fresh parsley

⅔ cup fresh lemon juice

Juice of ½ medium orange

2 tablespoons chopped fresh tarragon

4 (2-pound) live Maine lobsters

Salt and freshly ground black pepper

Fresh lemon wedges for garnish

For those of you who love all creatures and shudder when you see someone eating lobster, here are some "lobsta" facts: They have no vocal cords so they cannot "scream" when you cook them. They have a nervous system similar to that of a grasshopper and feel no pain. The best, most humane, way to speed their demise is to drown them in a sink full of tap water; just put them in the water and wait 5 minutes or so. They go to "sleep" and are then ready to cook.

Heat barbecue grill (or oven) to 400° F for grilling over direct heat.

In frying pan on grill or side burner, sauté shallots and garlic in olive oil for 5 minutes or until soft. Add butter, parsley, lemon and orange juice, and tarragon, and heat until the butter is melted. Set aside and keep warm, stirring occasionally.

Place each lobster on its back, sever the spinal cord by inserting a sharp knife between tail and body, and then split in half lengthwise. Remove stomach and intestinal vein, and rinse under running water to wash away the tomalley (unless, like me, you like its flavor). Remove and crack claws and sprinkle meat with salt and pepper, then brush with melted butter and put on the grill.

Paint lobster with melted butter mixture and put claws on the grill (covered). After 5 minutes, place the whole lobster on the grill flesh-side down, cooking in a covered grill until there is a light char on the meat, about 3 minutes Turn, baste with butter mixture, and grill just until the meat becomes firm, another 2–3 minutes. Claws should be done at the same time.

Remove lobsters and claws from grill and paint with melted butter mixture. Hit the back side of the claws with a large chef's knife to crack, and serve with the split lobsters. Garnish plates with lemon wedges.

Pork Tenderloins with Spicy Marmalade Glaze

SERVES 4-6

350°F
indirect grilling

2 (¾-pound) pork tenderloins

Salt and freshly ground
   black pepper

2 tablespoons flour

2 tablespoons extra-virgin
   olive oil

6 ounces lemonade concentrate,
   thawed (about ¾ cup)

3 tablespoons marmalade

¼ teaspoon cayenne pepper

1 teaspoon dry mustard

½ teaspoon dried thyme
   leaves

1 tablespoon brown sugar

If you're not a marmalade fan (some people don't like its bitter tang), you can substitute peach or apricot preserves, but I'd suggest adding a teaspoon of curry powder to give the fruit a bit more character.

Heat barbecue grill (or oven) to 350°F for grilling over indirect heat.

Spray tenderloins with nonstick grilling spray, then sprinkle generously with salt and pepper. Put the flour on a large flat plate, and coat all sides of the tenderloins with the flour.

Heat oil in a large cast-iron skillet or Dutch oven on barbecue grill or side burner. Brown the tenderloins in the skillet for about 5 minutes, turning to brown all sides.

In a large bowl, combine the lemonade, marmalade, cayenne, mustard, thyme, and brown sugar. Mix well and pour over the pork. Using tongs, turn the tenderloins to coat all sides, then bring to a simmer.

Place skillet on indirect side of the grill, cover the grill, and simmer for 20 minutes or until a thermometer inserted into the thickest portion of each tenderloin registers 145°F. Remove pork from the skillet, cover with foil, and let rest for 10 minutes.

Pour the sauce from the skillet into a sauceboat. Slice the pork into ¾-inch-thick slices and serve with the sauce on the side.

Good Doggies!

*I**nstead of using everyday, wrapped-in-plastic, mass-produced dogs, spend
a little cash and buy handmade dogs from your butcher shop or a gourmet
food store. If you can't find custom dogs, you can substitute bratwurst or Polish
sausage, but do try to get ones that aren't mass produced.*

Heat barbecue grill (or oven) to 375°F for grilling over direct heat.

Cut each hot dog almost in half lengthwise. Spread apart and brush
inside of each dog with mustard. Sprinkle with celery salt and pepper.

Grill bacon until it's just firm, drain, and cut into quarters (cut in half
lengthwise and widthwise). Fold each cheese slice in half lengthwise,
then fold in half lengthwise again. Place in hot dog, and put ¼ slice of
bacon on either side of the cheese. If using blue cheese, sprinkle some
inside the hot dog, then add the bacon.

Tie the hot dog partially closed in two places with butcher's twine.
Place dogs on grill with the cut-side up, covering loosely with a piece
of aluminum foil, shiny-side down. Cook until browned on bottom and
both sides, about 5–6 minutes.

While the hot dogs are cooking, mix the warm butter and minced garlic
together. Spread it on the hot dog buns and toast them on the grill.

Remove twine from dogs and serve them on the toasted buns.

SERVES 4-6

> 375°F
> direct grilling
> twine

**1 package of butcher shop
hot dogs**

**Dijon honey mustard (or
plain yellow mustard)**

Celery salt

Freshly ground black pepper

4 strips smoked bacon

**8 slices extra-sharp cheddar
cheese (or substitute
crumbled blue)**

Butcher's twine

**4 tablespoons (½ stick)
warm butter**

**1 teaspoon minced fresh
garlic**

Hot dog buns

Kobe Blue Burgers

425°F
direct grilling

1½ pounds ground sirloin
    Kobe beef (or ground chuck
    round)

¼ cup minced sweet onion

4 teaspoons favorite barbecue
    sauce

1 teaspoon balsamic vinegar

Salt and freshly ground
    pepper, to taste

4 tablespoons blue cheese

4 tablespoons (½ stick)
    butter, softened

1 tablespoon minced shallots

4 hamburger buns

After Japanese Kobe beef became popular, American ranchers decided to produce their own Kobe-style beef from Wagyu cattle crossbred with Angus cattle. Today, in a delightful turnaround, the American version is being imported to Japan.

Heat barbecue grill (or oven) to 425°F for grilling over direct heat.

Place the ground beef into a large bowl. Thoroughly mix the onion, barbecue sauce, vinegar, and salt and pepper into the beef. Shape a quarter of the mixture into a flat patty, then make a depression in center of patty and place 1 tablespoon blue cheese in the hole. Form meat around cheese to enclose it. Set aside, and make 3 more patties the same way.

Cook patties on hot, covered grill until done to your taste (please, no more than medium or, even better, medium-rare), about 3 minutes on first side, then 2–3 minutes on the second side.

While the patties are grilling, mix warm butter and minced shallots. Spread onto hamburger buns and grill until light brown. Serve the patties on the buns.

Buttermilk and Bacon Hush Puppies

Hush puppies have a colorful etymology, with four main theories of their origin: hunters or Confederate soldiers who both wanted to keep their dogs quiet when animals, or enemies, were nearby; a group of nuns in New Orleans who first cooked up the cornmeal treats; and an African cook who wanted to keep his puppy from crying as he fried some catfish. All but the nuns are alleged to have said (you guessed it): "hush puppies."

Heat barbecue grill or side burner to 350°F for grilling over direct heat.

In a large bowl, mix the cornmeal, flour, eggs, buttermilk, bacon, salt, pepper, baking powder, bacon fat, and brown sugar. Stir it all up until the ingredients are thoroughly blended.

Take a large spoonful of batter and roll it into a ping-pong size ball with your hands. Set the ball on a plate and continue making balls with the rest of the batter. If the batter is too sticky, add cornmeal, a tablespoonful at a time, until the balls hold together.

Heat 3 inches of oil in a Dutch oven placed directly on your barbecue grill or on a side burner. When a drop of water dropped into the oil sizzles, you've reached the right cooking temperature. Slide the balls into the hot oil using a long, slotted serving spoon. Allow them to brown on all sides, about 2–3 minutes. They should begin floating when done, but if they don't, be careful not to overcook them. They're ready when they're golden brown all over. Let hush puppies drain on a paper towel, then serve while still warm.

SERVES 4-6

> 350°F
> direct grilling

2 cups yellow cornmeal

1 cup all-purpose unbleached flour

2 eggs

1½ cups buttermilk

½ cup chopped cooked bacon pieces

¾ teaspoon seasoned salt

½ teaspoon ground pepper

3 teaspoons baking powder

2 tablespoons bacon fat

2 tablespoons brown sugar

Oil for deep frying

Grilled Garlic-Blue Bread

SERVES 6-8

350°F
direct grilling

1 (16-ounce) loaf of French
or Italian bread

8 tablespoons (1 stick)
unsalted butter, softened

2 large cloves garlic, minced

½ teaspoon garlic salt

2 tablespoons freshly
chopped parsley

¼ cup freshly grated Parmesan
cheese

3 tablespoons crumbled blue
cheese

How ow brave was the person who first decided to taste the cheese covered with mold retrieved from a dank cave in Roquefort-sur-Soulzon in the middle of France. "Mmmm, covered with blue mold, how yummy!" Produced today by injecting with Penicillium roqueforti *mold spores, blue cheese is considered one of the best and most flavorful in the world.*

Heat barbecue grill (or oven) to 350°F for grilling over direct heat.

Cut the bread in half, horizontally. In a medium bowl, mix together the softened butter, garlic, garlic salt, and parsley.

Spread butter mixture over the top and bottom halves of the bread. Place the bread, buttered-sides up, on a heavy-duty baking pan (do not use a cookie sheet) or on a barbecue griddle. Cook over direct heat in a covered grill for 10 minutes.

In a small bowl, combine the Parmesan and blue cheese and stir to mix.

Remove the pan from the barbecue and sprinkle the cheese mixture over the bread. Return to the barbecue and heat for additional 2–3 minutes until the edges of the bread begin to toast and the cheese begins to melt and bubble. The bread will quickly begin to burn on the edges, so watch carefully.

Remove the bread from the barbecue and let cool slightly, then cut into 2-inch-thick slices. Serve immediately.

Quadruple Cheese and Onion Potatoes

Not many people know that the air holes in Emmenthaler (in the U.S. it's called Swiss) cheese are caused by one strain of bacteria eating lactic acid, the waste product of other bacteria, then emitting CO2 gas, which forms the bubbles. Oops, pardon me, I bubbled!

Heat barbecue grill (or oven) to 350°F for grilling over direct heat.

In a medium bowl, mix the cheddar, mozzarella, Swiss, and Parmesan cheeses. Set ½ cup of the mixture aside.

In a large bowl, mix the potatoes and onions, then sprinkle with the bacon, chives, shallots, garlic salt, and several healthy grinds of pepper. Add the bulk of the grated cheese to the bowl, then gently mix together with a spatula.

Generously spray three pieces of heavy-duty foil (about 16 inches square) with nonstick cooking spray.

Place a third of the potato-cheese mixture onto each piece of foil, then place an equal number of butter slices on each pile. Fold each packet several times to seal in the potatoes, crimping ends to make sure they are tightly sealed.

Place the packets in the preheated grill, close barbecue lid, and cook for 35–40 minutes or until the potatoes are tender.

Remove the foil packets from the grill. Open each one carefully, so the steam that escapes doesn't burn you. Sprinkle the ½ cup reserved cheese mixture evenly over the three packets and add a dash or two of paprika for color.

SERVES 6-8

> 350°F
> direct grilling

½ cup (4 ounces) shredded sharp cheddar cheese

½ cup (4 ounces) shredded mozzarella cheese

½ cup (4 ounces) shredded Swiss or Emmenthaler cheese

⅓ cup grated Parmesan cheese

7 large potatoes, sliced ¼-inch thick

1 large onion, chopped

1 pound sliced bacon, cooked and crumbled

1 tablespoon minced fresh chives

1 tablespoon minced shallots

1 teaspoon garlic salt

Freshly ground black pepper

4 tablespoons (½ stick) butter, in ¼-inch slices

Paprika to garnish

Garlic, Herb, and Onion Potatoes

375°F
indirect grilling

6 large potatoes, unpeeled,
  cut in ½-inch-thick slices

6 medium onions, cut in
  ½-inch slices

½ teaspoon freshly ground
  pepper

1 tablespoon dried oregano

1 tablespoon minced garlic

1 teaspoon dried basil

¼ teaspoon dried savory

⅓ cup extra-virgin olive oil

½ cup grated Parmesan
  cheese

1 teaspoon paprika

member of the mint family, savory can be compared to thyme, oregano, or epazote and has sometimes been used as a substitute for pepper for those who need to avoid pepper because of allergies. It comes in both winter and summer varieties and is very popular in Italian cuisine. These potatoes are especially good with roasts, chops, and chicken or turkey.

Heat barbecue grill (or oven) to 375°F for grilling over indirect heat.

Place potatoes and onions in a shallow roasting pan.

In a small bowl, mix the pepper, oregano, garlic, basil, and savory.

Drizzle the potato and onion slices with olive oil and sprinkle with herb mixture. Toss to coat both sides.

Bake potato-herb mixture on indirect heat for about 1 hour (grill covered), or until potatoes are browned and tender, turning occasionally to keep them from sticking to the bottom of the pan. Remove pan from grill, sprinkle potatoes and onions with the Parmesan cheese, and stir so that all the slices are coated. Then sprinkle with the paprika as a decorative garnish.

Barbecue Fried Potatoes

*P*lease don't peel your taters! Eating spuds with the skin on is the way to go. Their brown suits contain vitamins C and B6 and are loaded with potassium (which helps maintain normal blood pressure). And for you antioxidant fans, the skins are full of carotenoids and anthocyanins — which I understand are good for you.

Heat barbecue grill (or oven) to 425°F for grilling over direct heat.

In a large bowl, mix the mustard, chile powder, cumin, salt, sage, and black pepper. Stir well.

Spray both sides of the potato slices with nonstick cooking spray, then sprinkle both sides with the mixed spices and arrange them in a single layer on a large baking sheet.

Barbecue for 45 minutes in a covered grill, turning potatoes once or twice, until they are browned on both sides and fork-tender. Remove from pan and keep warm until ready to serve.

SERVES 4-6

425°F
direct grilling

1 teaspoon dry mustard

¼ teaspoon chile powder

¼ teaspoon ground cumin

1 teaspoon salt

½ teaspoon dried sage

⅛ teaspoon freshly ground black pepper

6 large potatoes, unpeeled, cut into ¼-inch-thick slices

Cooking spray

Rice on the Grill

SERVES 4-6

> 350°F
> indirect grilling
> water pan

2 cups vegetable broth

1 cup uncooked long-grain
white rice

1 cup chopped onion

1 cup chopped, seeded
tomato

1 cup finely chopped red-
skinned apple, unpeeled

½ cup golden raisins

½ cup heavy cream

3 tablespoons butter,
cut into 4–5 pieces

1 tablespoon minced
fresh garlic

4 teaspoons mild curry
powder

1 tablespoon minced fresh
ginger

1 teaspoon ground coriander

1 teaspoon ground nutmeg

½ teaspoon ground cardamom

1½ teaspoons powdered
turmeric

½ teaspoon fine sea salt

Freshly ground black pepper

Fresh parsley, chopped, for
garnish

No, you don't pour the rice directly onto the grill! Those little white pieces would fall right through and burn up. This recipe calls for the rice to be folded into an airtight aluminum foil packet, which makes it a great dish for camping. Make at home, freeze, and place the packet right in your campfire coals.

Heat barbecue grill (or oven) to 350°F for grilling over indirect heat, with a water pan under the unheated side of the grill.

In a large bowl, mix together all the ingredients except the parsley until well combined.

Place a large sheet of heavy-duty aluminum foil on a cutting board and spoon the rice mixture into the center of the sheet, then fold up all edges with a double fold to seal well.

Slide the foil package onto the unheated side of the grill rack over the water pan.

Close the barbecue lid and cook for 15 minutes, then turn the foil package over and cook for an additional 15 minutes. Turn over again and cook for an additional 10 minutes. Carefully unseal one edge of the foil to check on the rice, being careful of the steam that will escape.

If rice is the right consistency, reseal the package and remove it from the grill. If rice is not tender enough, flip foil package one more time and cook for an additional 5 minutes. Let rice rest for 5 minutes before serving.

Using tongs and barbecue gloves and avoiding the steam, carefully open the foil package and spoon the rice mixture onto a heated serving dish. Sprinkle with parsley and serve.

Grilled Veggie Pitas

*P*ortobellos are merely grown-up brown crimini mushrooms that are lower in moisture, more flavorful, and meatier and much denser than their baby brothers. The name comes from: 1. a street in London; 2. a TV show; or 3. a translation of "large hat" in Italian.

Heat barbecue grill (or oven) to 350°F for grilling over direct heat.

Brush both sides of the eggplant, mushroom, bell peppers, and onion slices with a third of the salad dressing; sprinkle with salt and pepper; and let rest for 15 minutes.

Drain quickly and then grill (covered) until the vegetables have light grill marks on both sides and are crisp outside but tender inside, about 8–10 minutes. Remove from the grill and, on a cutting board, cut into small bite-size pieces. Place in a medium bowl, add the remaining dressing, and stir.

Cut pita bread in half and open the pockets. Fill each pita half with approximately 3 tablespoons of the grilled vegetables, sprinkle cheese on top of the veggies, and serve.

SERVES 4-6

350°F
direct grilling

1 large (16-ounce) eggplant, cut into ½-inch-thick slices

1 large (5- to 6-ounce) Portobello mushroom

1 medium red bell pepper, quartered

1 medium yellow or green bell pepper, quartered

1 large red onion, cut in ½-inch slices

½ cup Italian or honey-Dijon salad dressing

Sea salt and freshly ground black pepper

6 (8-inch) whole wheat or white pita breads

4 ounces shredded mozzarella-jack cheese blend

Crisp Veggie Patties

350°F
direct grilling

1 cup brown lentils

¼ cup minced carrots

3 cups vegetable stock

½ cup minced onions

¼ cup minced celery

¼ cup minced beets

2 tablespoons granulated garlic

3 tablespoons olive oil

½ cup fine breadcrumbs, fresh if possible

¼ cup all-purpose flour

2 tablespoons dry mustard

2 tablespoons minced fresh rosemary leaves

1 tablespoon minced fresh basil

½ teaspoon salt

¼ cup mayonnaise

1 teaspoon garlic powder

When shopping for lentils, look for ones that are clean, firm, dry, and not shriveled up, with uniform color. Brown lentils hold their shape through cooking much better than the red, orange, and yellow varieties.

Cook lentils and minced carrots in vegetable stock until soft, approximately 15 minutes. Drain and set aside.

In a medium saucepan over medium heat on side burner or stovetop, sauté the onions, celery, beets, and garlic in the olive oil until the onions are transparent, about 5 minutes. Lower the heat and add the lentil-carrot mixture, breadcrumbs, flour, mustard, rosemary, basil, and salt to the pan. Stir until a dough-like mass is formed, approximately 5 minutes.

Add more liquid if the dough is too dry, or add flour 1 teaspoon at a time if the dough is too moist. Using your hands, form the mixture into 8–10 patties and refrigerate them, covered, for 30–40 minutes.

Heat the barbecue grill (or oven) to 350°F for grilling over direct heat.

Grill the vegetable patties for approximately 4 minutes per side (grill covered), until they are just beginning to brown on both sides.

Mix mayonnaise and garlic powder. Serve with the vegetable patties.

Que'd Bean Skillet

SERVES 6-8

350°F
direct grilling

This dish is a feast for bean lovers: the pineapple and peaches, along with the stuffing cubes, give it a distinctive texture, and the molasses, cola, and mustard give it a tangy sweetness that goes perfectly with the spices of the Southern Pit recipe.

Heat barbecue grill (or oven) to 350°F for grilling over direct heat.

In a large mixing bowl, gently combine the beans, pineapple, stuffing cubes, peach, molasses, cola, onion, mustard, cumin, and chili sauce. Transfer mixture to a large cast-iron skillet. Cover the skillet with aluminum foil, put it into the barbecue, and bake, covered, for 30 minutes.

Remove the aluminum foil cover. Top the beans with rounds of refrigerated biscuits and bake, uncovered, for about 10 minutes longer, or until the biscuits puff up and are browned.

Serve from the skillet at the table, giving each person a biscuit and a heaping portion of beans.

3 (22-ounce) cans Bush's Southern Pit Barbecue beans

1 (14.5-ounce) can pinto beans, drained

1 cup chopped fresh pineapple

2 cups packaged stuffing cubes

1 large peach, chopped, skin left on

½ cup molasses

½ cup favorite cola (not diet cola)

1 large onion, roughly chopped

2 tablespoons Dijon mustard

½ teaspoon ground cumin

2 tablespoons chili sauce

1 (8-ounce) package ready-to-cook refrigerated biscuits

Tejano Corn Grill

400°F
direct grilling

6 ears corn on the cob,
unshucked (look for Peaches
& Cream variety)

½ cup mayonnaise

½ cup softened butter

1 teaspoon brown sugar

2 tablespoons fresh lime
juice

2 tablespoons ancho chile
powder

½ teaspoon garlic powder

½ teaspoon ground cumin

1 teaspoon freshly ground
black pepper

Peaches & Cream corn, also called Butter & Sugar corn, is usually only found in farmers' markets or for a very limited time in some grocery stores. The corn cob contains both yellow and white kernels and stays flavorful for up to 14 days after maturity. Some say it is the sweetest corn they have ever tasted. Once you've tried it, you'll be hooked.

Optional: Soak the corn in salted water for several hours to get the shucks moist. (Add 2 tablespoons salt per 1 gallon of water.)

Heat barbecue grill to 400°F for grilling over direct heat.

In a medium bowl, combine the mayonnaise, butter, sugar, lime juice, chile powder, garlic powder, cumin, and pepper. Stir until the ingredients are well mixed. Set aside for serving.

Grill the corn, with the shucks intact, over very hot coals on a charcoal grill or over high flames on a gas grill. Turn frequently until done, about 20–25 minutes. The corn is done when the shucks are well charred on all sides.

Wearing barbecue gloves, remove the shucks and the silk, which is easier to do after cooking than before. Serve the corn on a heated plate with the mayonnaise-butter spread and a pastry brush so guests can coat their own corn with as much of the spread as they wish.

Rum and Coke Cake

If you don't want to use alcohol in this recipe, you can substitute rum flavoring (which is more expensive). You will need to increase the cola to make up the difference in liquid flavorings. Put the 2 tablespoons of rum flavoring in a measuring cup and add cola to the ½ cup level. Do not substitute diet cola for the regular cola, since diet sodas tend to turn bitter when baked. This is a very rich and moist cake, so serve small slices.

Heat barbecue grill (or oven) to 350°F for grilling over indirect heat.

Grease and flour, or spray generously with a nonstick cooking spray, a 9x13-inch baking pan and set aside.

In a large bowl, combine flour and sugar and mix well.

In a medium saucepan, combine the cocoa, cola, rum, butter, and marshmallows. Bring to a boil, stirring frequently to mix. Pour the mixture into the bowl with the flour and sugar mixture and stir well.

In a separate bowl, mix the eggs, cream, lemon juice, and baking soda. Stir well. Then add to the bowl with the other ingredients, stir again, and pour batter into the prepared baking pan.

Place pan on double layer of aluminum foil on indirect heat side of grill.

Bake for about 30–35 minutes in a covered barbecue, until a toothpick inserted into the cake comes out clean. You do not need to rotate the cake while it is cooking.

While the cake is baking, make the frosting. In a large saucepan on a side burner or stovetop, mix the butter, cocoa, cola, and rum, and bring to a boil. Stir in the sugar, mixing well, then stir in the nuts. Keep warm. Remove cake from barbecue, let it cool for 20 minutes, and gently spread it with the warm frosting. Let cool before serving.

SERVES 10-12

350°F
indirect grilling

2 cups self-rising flour

2 cups brown sugar

¼ cup unsweetened cocoa powder

½ cup cola (Coca-Cola recommended; do not use diet cola)

½ cup dark rum (or 2 tablespoons rum flavoring)

1 cup (2 sticks) butter

1 cup miniature marshmallows

2 eggs, beaten

½ cup heavy cream

1 teaspoon fresh lemon juice

1 teaspoon baking soda

Frosting:

½ cup butter

2 tablespoons unsweetened cocoa powder

¼ cup cola (Coca-Cola recommended; do not use diet cola)

2 tablespoons dark rum (or 1 teaspoon rum flavoring)

1 (1-pound) box confectioners' sugar

½ cup chopped pecans or unsalted peanuts

Grilled Cherry Cobbler

SERVES 4-6

350°F
indirect grilling

8 tablespoons (1 stick)
  butter, melted

2 cups pitted sour cherries

¾ cup brown sugar

1 cup plus 1 tablespoon
  all-purpose flour

1 cup white sugar

1 teaspoon baking powder

1 cup whole milk

Topping:

½ cup brown sugar

¼ cup chopped pecans or
  unsalted peanuts

"Cobblers" get their name from the rough, "cobbled" surface of nuts-sugar-dough that is usually sprinkled on top. If you're not partial to cherries, you can make this with raspberries, blueberries, peaches, apricots, pluots, plums, or nectarines.

Preheat the barbecue to 350°F for grilling over indirect heat.

Pour melted butter into a preheated cast-iron skillet.

Place the cherries in a large bowl, and add the brown sugar and 1 tablespoon of flour. Gently toss with a spoon to coat all the cherries. Gently pour the cherries into the skillet so they are in a single layer.

In a medium bowl, stir the 1 cup flour with the white sugar and baking powder. Add milk and stir until blended, then pour the batter evenly into the pan over the cherries. Do not stir the mixture.

Bake for 20–25 minutes in the covered barbecue grill over indirect heat, until the batter becomes golden brown and a toothpick inserted into it comes out clean.

While the cobbler is baking, combine the topping ingredients and set aside. Remove finished cobbler from the grill and sprinkle with the sugar-nut topping.

Let cool and serve with vanilla ice cream or freshly whipped cream.

Brudder's Sweet Potato Pie

Don't use yams in this recipe; they're not interchangeable with sweet potatoes. Yams are related to grasses and lilies, while sweet potatoes are members of the morning glory family. Yams contain more moisture and are sweeter, while sweet potatoes contain more vitamins A and C. If you can't find sweet potatoes and must use yams, reduce the sugar to ¼ cup in the ingredients and topping.

Heat barbecue grill (or oven) to 350°F for grilling over indirect heat.

Put enough water in a medium-size pot to cover the sweet potatoes. Add ½ teaspoon salt. Bring the water to a boil, and then reduce heat to low. Cover the pot and let the sweet potatoes simmer for 20 minutes until soft.

Drain the water and mash the sweet potatoes in a large bowl.

In another bowl, beat the eggs with a fork, then add the milk, brown sugar, remaining ½ teaspoon salt, cinnamon, nutmeg, and melted butter. Mix well, then pour mixture into the bowl of mashed sweet potatoes. Mix again and pour into the prepared pie crust.

To prepare the topping, cream together the butter and brown sugar in a large bowl. Add the egg and, with a wire whisk, beat until the mixture is light and fluffy. Add the remaining ingredients, and whisk to blend well. Set aside.

Place the pie on the hot side of the grill over a 10-inch-square of heavy-duty aluminum foil (shiny-side down), and bake for 10 minutes. Move the pie to the cool side of the grill, pour the topping over it, and bake, covered, over indirect heat for 40–50 minutes until done and a toothpick inserted into center comes out clean.

SERVES 8-10

350°F
indirect grilling

1 pound sweet potatoes, peeled and cut in quarters

1 teaspoon salt

2 eggs

1½ cups evaporated milk

½ cup brown sugar

1 teaspoon ground cinnamon

½ teaspoon ground nutmeg

3 tablespoons butter, melted

1 (9-inch) deep pie crust

Praline topping:

2 tablespoons butter, softened

½ cup brown sugar

1 egg

1 cup chopped pecans

½ cup cane syrup (Steen's brand recommended)

Pinch of salt

½ tablespoon grated orange zest

½ teaspoon ground cinnamon

Blueberry-Raspberry-Strawberry Lasagna

9 precooked lasagna noodles

15 ounces ricotta cheese

⅔ cup white sugar

1 large egg

1 cup all-purpose flour

1 cup well-packed brown
sugar

1 teaspoon ground cinnamon

½ teaspoon ground nutmeg

Pinch of ground cloves

Pinch of chile powder

½ cup butter, melted

1 pint raspberries

1 pint strawberries, sliced

1 pint blueberries

Freshly whipped cream or
vanilla ice cream for serving

While this dessert pasta may sound odd, once you've tried it you'll be hooked. You can substitute sliced peaches and nectarines, slices of tart apples, or even fresh apricot slices in this recipe. If using berries, be sure to let the dessert cool before serving, as the berries get very hot and can burn your mouth.

Heat barbecue grill (or oven) to 350°F for grilling over indirect heat.

Lay 3 cooked lasagna noodles in the bottom of 9-inch-square metal baking pan you've buttered or coated with nonstick cooking spray.

In a large bowl, combine the ricotta cheese, white sugar, and egg, and beat until almost smooth.

In a separate bowl, combine the flour, brown sugar, cinnamon, nutmeg, cloves, chile powder, and melted butter. Mix well.

Gently fold the raspberries and strawberries into the blueberries, being careful not to crush the raspberries.

Top the first layer of lasagna noodles with one-third of the berry mixture, followed by one-third of the flour-sugar-spice mixture and one third of the cheese-sugar-egg mixture.

Repeat, adding two more layers of all three components.

Bake for 45 minutes over indirect heat in covered barbecue grill, until the top is golden brown and the filling is bubbling. Remove, cool for 10–15 minutes, and then serve with fresh whipped cream or vanilla ice cream.

Fall Recipes

Traditional Smoke-Barbecued Turkey

350°/300°F
direct grilling
16–24 hours brining
wood chips
drip pan
V-rack

Brine:

7 cups hot water

1 cup kosher salt

2 cups apple cider

1 cup brown sugar
  (or maple syrup)

3 tablespoons red pepper
  flakes

1 (20- to 22-pound) fresh
  or fully thawed turkey

10 pounds ice cubes

Extra-virgin olive oil

Your favorite stuffing

Rub:

1 tablespoon sea salt

1 teaspoon freshly ground
  black pepper

4 tablespoons poultry
  seasoning

¼ teaspoon cayenne pepper

Gravy fixings:

3½ cups stock

6 tablespoons flour

Pinch of salt

*B*rines are salted solutions used to add moisture and help tenderize poultry and meats. Food that is brined stays juicy and tender during grilling or smoking. Sugar, spices, salt, and herbs are usually added to the brine to enhance flavor.

In a large saucepan, stir the hot water and salt together until the salt is dissolved. Add the apple cider, brown sugar, and red pepper, and stir well. Pour the warm liquid into a large aluminum or plastic container (a 30-quart turkey frying pot is perfect), add 10 pounds of ice cubes (the usual size most grocery stores sell of packaged ice cubes), and stir.

Place the turkey in the container, cover with a lid or plastic wrap held on with twine, and let it brine for at least 16 hours (I typically brine it for 24 hours). You can, if you must, even put the bird in the brine frozen and allow it to thaw in the brine.

After brining, heat barbecue grill (or oven) to 350˚F for grilling over direct heat. (I use a Big Green Egg grill and highly recommend it for cooking turkeys, and just about everything else. Most of what follows is easily applicable to any charcoal grill, however.)

In a small bowl, mix the rub ingredients together, cover, and set aside. Soak a few handfuls of flavored wood chips (apple is best, but you can also use cherry, pecan, or hickory) in water for 1 to 2 hours.

Pull turkey from the brine, rinse it off and pat dry, rub with olive oil, and then season with the rub, both outside and inside the bird. Fill both body cavities with your favorite stuffing, sewing up the rear cavity with poultry skewers and twine. (I just mound the stuffing in the main cavity, not worrying about closing it.)

Just before you put the turkey on the grill, toss a handful of the soaked wood chips on the coals. Place a drip pan on the grill, set a V-rack inside the pan, add ½ inch of water, and place the turkey on the V-rack.

Close vents or open the lid to reduce the temperature to 300˚F. As needed, add already lit charcoal, briquettes, or wood for your brand of barbecue. It's a good idea, though, to leave the exhaust vent all the way open to avoid too much smoke building up in the grill. Add more fuel as needed to maintain the temperature, and add one more handful of soaked wood chips to try to keep a nice light flow of smoke passing over the turkey.

You should turn the bird 180 degrees about 1½ hours into the cooking

time to ensure even cooking. Brush the skin 3 or 4 times with drippings from the drip pan.

A 20- to 22-pound bird usually will cook between 4½–5 hours at an ideal temperature of between 250–300°F. On average it takes about 20 minutes a pound.

When a meat thermometer inserted in the thigh reaches 175–180°F, remove the turkey, cover it with foil, and let it rest for 20 minutes before carving.

Pour the drippings into a glass measuring cup. Wait until fat rises to the top and spoon it off, reserving 6 tablespoons. Pour the remaining drippings back into the roasting pan, add the reserved fat, stock, and flour, a pinch of salt, and whisk over heat until gravy thickens. Pour into a sauceboat and keep warm.

Remove stuffing first, place in bowl, cover, set aside and keep warm, then carve ol' Tom.

Serve with your favorite side dishes and the gravy you've made from the drippings.

Carolina-Style Barbecue Turkey

SERVES 8-10

> 350°F
> indirect grilling
> water pan

1 (10- to 12-pound) whole
turkey, fresh or fully
thawed

½ cup olive oil or other
cooking oil

Salt and freshly ground
black pepper

1½ pounds smoked bacon

Carolina-style barbecue
sauce:

2 cups apple cider vinegar

1 tablespoon crushed red
pepper flakes

½ cup brown sugar

1 cup water

Bread rolls or hamburger
buns for serving

If you desire a spicier version of the Eastern North Carolina–style barbecue sauce, I suggest you add a tablespoon of hot pepper sauce. If you add ketchup or Worcestershire sauce, you're serving Western North Carolina–style sauce.

Heat barbecue grill (or oven) to 350°F for grilling over indirect heat, with large water pan under unheated side.

Cut the turkey in half down the breastbone and rub the skin on both halves with oil. Season with salt and pepper, then wrap with bacon slices. (If the turkey is larger than 12 pounds, use bacon substitute such as ¼-inch-thick slices of pork fatback, as real bacon will burn in the time it takes to cook a large bird.)

Place the turkey halves, breast-side up, on grill rack over the water pan. Grocery stores sell large aluminum roasting pans that are big enough for 2 turkey halves. Close lid of barbecue and grill turkey for 2½–3 hours, brushing with olive oil 2 or 3 times during the cooking process.

The turkey is done when a meat thermometer inserted into deepest portion of thigh reaches 170°F and the leg bone will turn and separate from meat. Turkey should be golden brown. Remove turkey from the grill and loosely tent with foil; temperature in bird will actually rise 10 degrees. Let cool to room temperature. Remove the turkey meat from the bones and loosely chop, shred, or slice. Add salt and pepper to taste, and mix well.

Mix vinegar, crushed red pepper flakes, brown sugar, and water. Add more water if vinegar mixture is too strong. Sprinkle half of the sauce over the chopped turkey and stir gently. Serve with large bread rolls or hamburger buns and the rest of the vinegar-pepper barbecue sauce.

The American Turkey (Meleagris gallopavo)

A DUMB BIRD IS HE

The domesticated turkey is perhaps the dumbest creature on the planet, next to perhaps gooney birds, goldfish, and lawn mold.

But it's not their fault. It's because they've been bred, and rebred, and breaded some more, generation after generation, in captivity. Darwin's Laws of Natural Selection and Variation don't work when some bozo wearing horn-rimmed glasses and thongs feeds you, raises you, protects you, houses you, nurtures you, and then hacks off your head.

To be kind, one can say that turkeys lack "street savvy," or in this case even "turkey-pen savvy."

But over and above that, they're fat, weak, and probably couldn't fend for themselves if they were allowed to fend. They're clumsy, they're slower than a three-legged turtle, and, in a bid to prevent escape from that turkey pen, each and every last one of 'em has been bred to forget how to fly. Sad to say, they ain't good for much besides, thank the Lord, good eatin'.

When Benjamin Franklin was arguing their merit, comparing them to the eagle for consideration as the national bird, he opined:

> For the Truth the Turkey is in Comparison a much more respectable Bird, and withal a true original Native of America... He is besides, though a little vain & silly, a Bird of Courage, and would not hesitate to attack a Grenadier of the British Guards who should presume to invade his Farm Yard with a red Coat on.

But we continue our dissing of the bird anyway. Turkeys are insecure, panic easily, and get "all het up" at the slightest change in their environment. Watch what happens in a flock of turkeys if you make a loud noise — instant bedlam, almost like a 95 percent discount sale in lady's shoes at Nordstrom's Rack.

If there were turkey psychologists, they'd make a fortune. When frightened, gazillions of frantic and frenetic birds run around in circles and flee smack-dab into the nearest corner, wooden fence, or barn. And then dozens more birds behind them charge full speed into the same corner, fence, or barn and everyone ends up in a big pile of broken turkeys — the maimed and crippled ones on top smothering those even unluckier birds at the bottom.

And guess what else? Turkeys have heart attacks. The United States Air Force was doing test runs and breaking the sound barrier near a turkey farm, where hundreds of turkeys dropped dead from heart attacks.

Urban legend aside, there are somewhat reliable, if you believe the old "I-know-people-who-know-people-who-saw-them," kinda stories of young birds opening their thirsty mouths to raindrops pouring from the sky, but forgetting to close them and drowning in one last quench of thirst. But we don't believe those stories....naaaa!

By the way, the bird's name is another mistake. A long time ago, some folks thought the funny looking birds came from — you guessed it — Turkey, when really they'd been here (ask your neighborhood Pilgrim) for years. But some dolt somehow got the idea that turkeys were guinea fowl that came from Islamic "Turkish" lands, and passed that brilliant deduction on to someone else. Like a culinary game of "telephone." Oops.

A few experts think the Pilgrims, sometime between September and November of 1621, served the first Thanksgiving dinner. Or was it in July 1623? Or was it November 1621? You get the idea, no one really knows. Others credit the settlers of Virginia's Jamestown with celebrating the first Thanksgiving as their version of England's ancient Harvest Home Festival, since there were no Bowl games to watch. I don't think there were, anyway. Pigskins then mainly stayed on the pig.

And still another group of historians, who happened to be sitting in Newt's Olde Tyme Taverne swigging Rolling Rock, swear that a guy named Morris Butterball started it all when he invited a few Pilgrim friends over for beer and some sorta bird. Oh yeah, Pilgrims didn't drink beer; in that case, he probably gave 'em a second helping of lime Jell-O mold and another frozen crescent roll.

President Abraham Lincoln proclaimed Thanksgiving a national holiday in 1863, supposedly as a response to a campaign organized by a feisty magazine editor, Sara Joseph Hale.

From 1846 to 1863, Ms. Hale, the editor of Godey's Lady Book, a sort of Ladies' Home Journal of the 1800s, and the author of "Mary Had a Little Lamb," embarked on a campaign to turn Thanksgiving into a national holiday during which workers would not be required to go to work. Yay, Sara!

Her campaign resulted in Lincoln's Thanksgiving proclamation — the first such proclamation of a national Thanksgiving holiday since 1789, when George W. (the first George W. to become president) proclaimed a National Day of Thanksgiving, a holiday that was dropped by subsequent presidents. Maybe they didn't like turkey, or days off.

But after Lincoln's rescue of the day, Thanksgiving has been celebrated as a national holiday, an American celebration of football, a big parade in front of New York (and Chicago) department stores, the birth date of John Madden's six-legged turkeys, and a day in late November when we don't have to work. Thanks again, Sara. And Abe.

In 1939 President Franklin Roosevelt moved Thanksgiving from the last Thursday to the third Thursday in November. He wanted to help business (malls, Wal-Mart, and Costco, and online Web sites of the day) by lengthening the shopping period before Christmas. Today that shopping period only seems to have grown to run from July 5th until Christmas.

In 1941 this unpopular move (Frankie's Turkeygate?) inspired Congress to permanently fix the date on the fourth Thursday of November.

In the year 2007, about 267,685,000 million turkeys were raised in the U.S., and it's estimated that 29 percent of those unfortunate birds are consumed during the holidays. After all, that dumb bird really, really tastes good.

Through the years, these dates have been circled in black on turkey calendars all over the country, and those few turkeys lucky enough to see the following day's sunrise count themselves as really, really lucky.

There are very few really, really lucky turkeys.

Cajun Deep-Fried Turkey

SERVES 8-10

kitchen syringe
large fryer (30- to 32-quart)
with basket or holder

Injection marinade:

1 cup Italian dressing
(important that it be
strained)

¼ cup Louisiana hot sauce

2 tablespoons liquid smoke

1 teaspoon garlic powder

2 tablespoons seasoned salt

Water

Canal Street rub:

1 teaspoon cayenne pepper

1 teaspoon curry powder

1 teaspoon powdered
turmeric

1 teaspoon ground ginger

1 teaspoon ground cumin

1 tablespoon chile powder

1 tablespoon paprika

Dash of nutmeg

10- to 12-pound turkey,
defrosted

Peanut oil for deep frying

I know this isn't a barbecue or grilling recipe, but folks sure do love to fry up a turkey now and then, especially during the holidays. So read carefully, follow instructions especially regarding the burner and flame, and enjoy! I recommend marinating the turkey for at least a full 24 hours, if not 2 to 3 days before deep frying. I put the turkey in a 30- or 32-quart pot and cook it over a gas flame burner.

Mix the marinade ingredients together, then add enough water to make 1 quart of marinade.

Mix the rub ingredients in a small bowl and set aside.

Remove giblets from turkey, wash the bird and pat dry, especially inside the cavity. Using a kitchen syringe, inject the turkey with the marinade in multiple locations in each breast and each thigh/leg. Rub inside cavity and the complete outside of the bird with the seasoning rub. Refrigerate turkey for at least 24 hours, but if you can, place in a plastic garbage bag and seal, then refrigerate for 2–3 days.

You need to measure the amount of oil before pouring it into the deep fryer. Place turkey in empty pot, pour in water until turkey is covered by about an inch, then remove turkey and dry it thoroughly. Mark the remaining water level in the pot with a marker or crayon, pour out the water, dry the pot thoroughly, add oil to the mark, and begin heating.

Using a frying thermometer, heat peanut oil in deep fryer to 360°F.

Place bird on turkey basket or holder. SHUT OFF FLAME. Slowly lower into the oil, stopping and lifting it slightly as needed to prevent splattering, until the bird is submerged. TURN FLAME BACK ON.

Cook 3–4 minutes per pound. DO NOT LEAVE THE POT UNATTENDED WHILE COOKING. When turkey reaches the proper temperature (breast 160°F, thigh 175°F), TURN FLAME OFF. Slowly lift the turkey out of the pot and drain it on paper towels. Let the oil in the pot cool down at least an hour before you try to move it.

Let turkey sit for 5 minutes, then carve and enjoy.

Cornish Apple Cider Game Hens

SERVES 4-6

> 350°F
> indirect grilling
> water pan
> marinate overnight

Marinade:

3 cups apple juice or cider

1 tablespoon brown sugar

1 teaspoon minced garlic

1 teaspoon balsamic vinegar

½ teaspoon crushed red pepper flakes

2 Cornish game hens (about 1¼–1½ pounds each)

Olive oil

Dry rub:

1 tablespoon granulated garlic

1 tablespoon brown sugar

1 teaspoon dried thyme

1 teaspoon dried savory

1 teaspoon ground cumin

1 teaspoon sea salt

1 teaspoon white pepper

1 teaspoon paprika

Sauce:

½ cup apple cider

¼ cup cider vinegar

½ cup smoky bbq sauce

¼ cup cane syrup

They aren't Cornish, they're not wild game birds, and half of them aren't hens. They are merely young chickens (5–6 weeks old) of both sexes that weigh in at less than 2 pounds.

Mix the marinade ingredients in a resealable 2-quart plastic bag, and shake until well mixed. Add the Cornish hens. Leave the sealed bag in a bowl in the refrigerator overnight, turning bag several times during the marinating process.

Heat barbecue grill (or oven) to 350°F for grilling over indirect heat, with water pan under unheated side.

Mix the dry rub ingredients in a small bowl.

Remove Cornish hens from marinade, wash, then pat them dry. Brush with olive oil, then season them generously inside and out with the rub. Work the mixture well into the skin and under the skin wherever possible. Place in a large bowl, cover, and leave at room temperature for 20–30 minutes.

Cook hens over unheated side of the grill, covered, for 45 minutes to 1 hour or until they brown nicely and the internal temperature of the thigh reaches 180°F. Remove the hens from the grill and let them rest for 10 minutes.

While hens are cooking, mix the sauce in a medium saucepan. While stirring, heat the mixture to boiling, then lower the heat to a medium simmer, and reduce the liquid in the pan to a third of the original volume, or until it's thick enough to lightly coat a spoon.

Halve each of the hens and serve with the warm barbecue sauce.

Prime Rib Baked in Salt

SERVES 8-10

> 450°F
> direct grilling
> spray bottle

1 (8- to 9-pound, 5- to 6-rib) prime rib roast (small end of the prime, chine removed)

¼ cup Worcestershire sauce

1 tablespoon salt

2 teaspoons freshly ground black pepper

2 tablespoons crushed rosemary

2 tablespoons dried oregano

3 large garlic cloves, thinly sliced

3-4 boxes (3 pounds each) kosher salt (Morton's recommended)

Cold water

A prime rib roast cooked without a salt crust comes out rare in the center, loses lots of its natural juices in the roasting pan, and often has a very dark and dry outside. The salt in this recipe seals in all the juices and keeps the outside of the roast moist, but it does not impart a salty taste to the meat. Since the salt keeps all the juices inside the roast, it may look more rare (pink) than if you cook it another way. The secret is cooking to the right internal temperature.

Heat barbecue grill (or oven) to 450°F for grilling over direct heat.

Using a very sharp knife, cut into the fat layer at the top of the meat, but do not cut it off. Merely cut a flap so that the rub can be placed on the meat, and the fat layer can be folded back over to cover the meat.

Rub the outside of the prime rib all over with Worcestershire sauce, covering well. Sprinkle with the salt, black pepper, rosemary, and oregano. Cut slits all over the meat, inserting a slice of garlic into each slit.

Line a large roasting pan with aluminum foil, then pour a layer of kosher salt in the pan about 1 inch deep. Using a spray bottle, lightly wet the salt. Then lay the prime rib in the pan on the salt, fat-side up.

Mix the remaining salt with enough water to form a slightly stiff paste, which will help it form a solid crust. Cover the prime rib completely with the salt paste, at least ¼-inch thick, and, while the salt is still soft, insert a meat thermometer into the center of the roast through the salt.

Open the vents in the grill, which will eventually reduce the temperature to about 325°F. Place the roasting pan in the center of the grill, close lid, and cook for about 2–2½ hours, or until the meat thermometer reads 130°F. The meat thermometer is IMPORTANT, as different thicknesses of salt, and a zillion other factors will influence the time that the roast cooks.

Take the roasting pan out of the grill and let the meat sit for 20–25 minutes. Then, with a hammer, break the salt covering. Be careful not to burn yourself on the very hot salt. Remove the roast from the salt crust and thoroughly brush off any remaining salt. Place on a heated platter and slice.

Porterhouse Pork Chops with Blackberry Cabernet Sauce

SERVES 4-6

> 400°F
> direct grilling
> 4- to 24-hour seasoning

¼ cup Dijon-honey mustard

4 (16-ounce) porterhouse
pork chops

Rub:

1 teaspoon dried sage

½ teaspoon salt

2 tablespoons brown sugar

¼ teaspoon paprika

1 tablespoon garlic powder

Sauce:

3 cups fresh blackberries

¼ cup good Cabernet wine

1 cup sugar

2 tablespoons rice wine
vinegar

2 tablespoons butter

Fresh rosemary sprigs for
garnish

Chops aren't just chops. Several varieties could be used in this recipe: Loin, butterfly loin, rib, sirloin, top loin, and loin blade chops are all good choices. But to make a lasting impression, buy porterhouse pork chops (at least 1½ inches thick), chops that have a bone down the center with the sirloin portion on one side and the fillet portion on the other.

Massage the mustard into the chops. Combine all rub ingredients in a bowl. Sprinkle rub on the pork chops, coating them evenly, then pat rub lightly into the meat. Put on a plate, cover with plastic wrap, and refrigerate from 4–24 hours.

Heat barbecue grill (or oven) to 400°F for grilling over direct heat.

In a small saucepan, mash the berries, cover them with wine and poach for 10 minutes over low heat.

In separate saucepan, heat the sugar and vinegar and simmer 2–3 minutes. Pour into the berry-wine mixture and reduce over low heat until syrupy, about 20–30 minutes. Sauce should be tangy. Set aside.

Let chops come up to room temperature, then grill them (covered), 5–6 inches over glowing coals or gas flames, for 4–5 minutes on each side, or until a meat thermometer diagonally inserted into the center of each chop registers 145°F.

Remove the chops from the grill and seal them in heavy-duty foil. Let stand 8–10 minutes before serving.

Just before serving, whisk in 2 tablespoons butter to smooth the warm sauce. Serve the chops with the warmed sauce. Garnish the chops with sprigs of fresh rosemary or sage.

Grilled Rib Eye Steaks with Roquefort Butter

Most barbecue cooks and steakhouse chefs agree that by far the best steak to grill is the rib eye, also called the Delmonico and Scotch Fillet. It's popular because it's more tender, juicy, and marbled than just about any other steak. It's best cooked and served bone-in, as the moisture and fat along the bone adds to the flavor.

Heat barbecue grill (or oven) to 450°F for direct heating.

Rub olive oil generously onto both sides of the steak and liberally season each side with freshly ground pepper.

Place the steaks in a preheated cast-iron skillet on the grill and cook for 2–3 minutes per side.

Remove the steaks, place them in an oven-proof skillet or on a baking sheet, and return to the barbecue. Cook, covered, for 5–10 minutes more for medium-rare steaks (135°F internal temperature), or longer for medium (150°F) or medium-well (155°F).

While the steaks are cooking, mash together the butter, crumbled Roquefort cheese, shallots, and brandy. Season with salt and pepper.

Remove the steaks from the pan and place them on a heated platter, top each cooked steak with a generous portion of the Roquefort butter, cover with foil, and let rest for 10 minutes. Watch as the internal temperature rises to 145°F — a perfect medium-rare! Or 160°F for medium or 165–170°F for medium-well. Personally, I do not recommend anything over 160°F. Serve immediately.

SERVES 4-6

> 450°F
> direct grilling

4 (or 6) rib eye steaks,
  1–1¼ inches thick
  (8–10 ounces each)
Extra-virgin olive oil
Freshly ground black pepper

Roquefort butter:
1 stick (8 tablespoons)
  unsalted butter, at room
  temperature
4-6 tablespoons Roquefort
  (or blue) cheese, crumbled
½ teaspoon finely minced
  shallots
2 teaspoons brandy
Salt
Freshly ground black pepper

Satay-Stuffed Pork Loin

SERVES 6-8

> 350°F
> direct/indirect grilling
> twine

1 cup peanut butter (crunchy
is best)

¼ cup finely chopped
unsalted peanuts

¼ cup sesame oil

3 tablespoons molasses

¼ teaspoon dried thyme

⅛ teaspoon ground cloves

¼ teaspoon ground cumin

2 teaspoons minced fresh
garlic

3 tablespoons soy sauce

½ cup packed dark brown
sugar

1 (5- to 6-pound) boneless
loin of pork

¼ cup minced green onions,
white and green parts

Olive oil

Salt and freshly ground
black pepper

If you aren't a satay (peanut sauce) fan, you can substitute dried apricots, plums, raisins, apple slices, or peaches by chopping them in a food processor, then spreading the paste over the meat in the same manner as described below.

Heat barbecue grill to 350°F for grilling over direct and indirect heat.

Mix the peanut butter, peanuts, sesame oil, molasses, thyme, cloves, cumin, garlic, soy sauce, and brown sugar in a food processor. Pulse until you have a thick paste.

Cut the loin into a ½-inch-thick roll by cutting into the length of the meat ½-inch deep, then cut parallel to the outside surface all the way to the middle, unrolling the meat as you cut until you have a ½-inch-thick roast that looks like an unrolled cake roll.

With a spatula or butter knife, spread the peanut paste on the surface of the meat, covering it completely. Sprinkle the green onions over all. Roll up roast lengthwise very tightly and tie in 3 or 4 places with butcher's twine. Let the meat sit in refrigerator for 20 minutes.

Place a round piece of aluminum foil, which you've cut to size, over the ends of the roast. Tie it on crosswise with two pieces of twine to hold it tightly over the ends, so that the inside stuffing won't leak out.

Brush the outside of the roast with olive oil and liberally salt and pepper the meat. Place the roast on the direct side of grill rack for 3–5 minutes per side to sear the meat, then move to the indirect side, cut-side up, and cook for 1–1½ hours in a covered grill until the internal temperature reaches 155–160°F.

Transfer roast to a large platter or cutting board, and let it rest, covered with foil, for 15 minutes. Discard the twine and aluminum foil and cut roast into ½-inch slices to serve.

Grilled Giant Scallops with Mandarin Orange–Lime Sauce

SERVES 6-8

350°F
direct grilling
wood chips
flat metal skewers

Sauce:

¼ cup mandarin orange juice

Juice of 1 lime

1½ teaspoons cider vinegar

1 small shallot, minced

1 tablespoon cracked peppercorns

Pinch of salt

2 tablespoons heavy cream

8 tablespoons (1 stick) butter, cut in small cubes

2 pounds large (10/20) sea scallops

2 tablespoons olive oil

¼ teaspoon salt

⅛ teaspoon freshly ground black pepper

Mandarin orange segments for garnish

Rosemary sprig for garnish

When you buy scallops, ask for "non-chem" or "dry pack," which means the seafood is "chemical free" and "unsoaked" (to avoid unscrupulous retailers who add phosphates and water to increase the weight by up to 25 percent). Use 10/20 size, meaning there are 10–20 scallops per pound; U-10 (10 per pound) are better but are very expensive and hard to find.

About an hour before you plan to eat, soak a handful of apple, cherry, or other fruitwood chips in water.

In a small saucepan, over medium heat, combine the mandarin orange juice, lime juice, vinegar, shallots, cracked pepper, and salt. Cook for 5 minutes, stirring. Add the heavy cream and continue cooking until reduced by half, then reduce the heat to medium-low. Gradually drop in the butter a few pieces at a time, and stir until the butter has melted. Remove the pan from the heat, pour the sauce into a sauceboat, and keep warm.

Heat barbecue grill (or oven) to 350˚F for grilling over direct heat.

Trim the small rectangular muscles from each scallop, then rinse the scallops, pat them dry, and place them on two or three flat, metal skewers. Brush with olive oil and season with salt and pepper.

Scatter the soaked wood chips over the flames or coals and heat until smoking. Then place the skewers on the grill and close the grill lid.

Cook only until lightly golden and opaque, about 2½–3 minutes, then turn and lightly brown the second side for 2 minutes. Slide the scallops onto a serving platter and garnish with mandarin orange segments and a sprig of rosemary. Serve immediately with sauce on the side.

Stuffed Baked Whole Salmon

350°F
direct grilling
twine

4 slices smoked bacon

½ cup diced onion

1 tablespoon minced garlic

1 pound cooked Dungeness crabmeat (or small cooked cocktail shrimp)

2 tablespoons chopped fresh parsley

1 tablespoon chopped fresh sage

1 teaspoon ground dried oregano

½ teaspoon freshly ground black pepper

½ teaspoon brown sugar

½ teaspoon sea salt flakes

1 whole salmon, about 5–5½ pounds, scaled, boned for stuffing

Salt and pepper

1 large lemon, seeded, cut in 5 or 6 thin slices

Extra-virgin olive oil

The best-tasting salmon are those that live in the wild. Their rich flavor is much preferred to freshwater or farmed varieties. Even their color, which comes from the crustaceans and insects they feed on, is brighter, pinker, and more vivid. Whenever possible, try to buy American Pacific wild salmon; the Atlantic wild varieties mainly come from Canada and Europe.

With a sharp knife, dice the bacon into very small pieces and cook in a skillet over low heat until lightly browned, about 2–3 minutes. Add the onion and garlic and sauté until onion is translucent and garlic softens, about 5 minutes. Remove the skillet from the heat.

Add the cooked crabmeat, parsley, sage, oregano, pepper, brown sugar, and salt flakes. Stir well, put in a bowl, cover, and chill in refrigerator.

Heat barbecue grill to 350°F for grilling over a sheet of heavy-duty aluminum foil over direct heat.

Lay the salmon on a cutting board. Open the cavity and lightly season the flesh with salt and pepper. Place the lemon slices (leaving a handful for garnish) along one side of the salmon, and spread the chilled crabmeat stuffing on top of the lemon slices. Fold the other side of the salmon over the stuffing and tie the fish closed with butcher's twine. Cover the tail and head with foil, then brush the skin on both sides with olive oil.

Place the tied salmon on the foil and cook for 30–40 minutes, turning once halfway through. Remove the salmon from the grill, remove head and tail coverings, loosely tent with another sheet of aluminum foil, and let it rest for 10 minutes before serving.

Cut the strings and remove. Serve everyone a portion of fish and stuffing, garnished with a slice of lemon.

Sweet Potato Biscuits

*M*ost sweet potatoes grown in the U.S. hail from Mississippi, North Carolina, California, and Louisiana, where 1.8 billion pounds are produced in one year alone. You can use yams in this recipe but if you do, cut the brown sugar in half as they are sweeter than sweet potatoes.

Heat barbecue grill (or oven) to 425°F for grilling over direct heat.

Melt the butter in a small saucepan, and set aside to cool.

In a large bowl, sift together both flours, then sift in the baking powder and stir in the salt.

In a separate bowl, stir the cooled butter into the mashed sweet potatoes, blending well. Add the brown sugar and beaten eggs, and stir the mixture well to blend. Add the dry ingredients, a cupful at a time, and stir to blend well. Turn the dough onto a floured board and knead briefly. If dough is too sticky, add more flour, a tablespoon at a time, until right consistency is reached.

Roll the dough to ½-inch thickness, and then use a 2-inch-round cookie cutter to cut out biscuits, placing them on a lightly greased baking sheet. Gather up the remaining scraps and reroll to a ½-inch thickness. Continue to cut out biscuits until no dough remains. There should be 12–14 biscuits.

Bake in the preheated barbecue (covered) until golden, about 9–11 minutes.

SERVES 4-6

425°F
direct grilling

2 tablespoons butter

1½ cups all-purpose unbleached flour

1½ cups cake flour

1 tablespoon baking powder

1 teaspoon salt

1½ cups mashed baked sweet potatoes

¼ cup brown sugar

2 large eggs, beaten

Blue Moon Corn Muffins

425°F
indirect grilling

1½ cups sifted all-purpose
  unbleached flour

2¼ teaspoons baking powder

¾ teaspoon salt

1 tablespoon sugar

¾ cup yellow cornmeal

¼ cup fresh or frozen
  (thawed) corn kernels

½ cup crumbled blue cheese

2 eggs, beaten

1 tablespoon honey

1 cup milk

4 tablespoons (½ stick)
  butter, melted

For an interesting variation to this recipe, instead of whole kernel corn, use ½ cup creamed corn and reduce milk to ¾ cup. Or, you can use buttermilk instead of milk.

Heat barbecue grill (or oven) to 425˚F for grilling over indirect heat.

Grease a muffin pan; set aside.

Combine the flour, baking powder, salt, and sugar, and then stir in the cornmeal, corn kernels, and crumbled blue cheese.

Make a well in center of the dry ingredients. Add the beaten eggs, honey, milk, and the melted butter; stir just until the dry ingredients are incorporated.

Fill the muffin cups two-thirds full with batter. Bake in the covered barbecue for 20–25 minutes, or until the tops of the muffins are nicely browned.

Wild Rice, Cranberry, and Apricot Stuffing

*D*ried cranberries first appeared in markets in the 1980s, and are heavily sweetened to counteract the natural sour taste of the raw fruit. You can, if you wish, substitute raisins or currents in this recipe, but if so I prefer the golden variety of raisins. This stuffing is great in chicken, pork chops, turkey, game hens, or rolled-up fish fillets.

Heat barbecue grill to 350°F for grilling over indirect heat.

Cook rice with stock and seasoned salt in a medium saucepan, covered, over direct heat on the covered grill for 60 minutes or until the grains begin to split. Drain rice in a wire-mesh colander and allow to cool.

Melt butter in a small skillet, and then add the shallots and garlic. Sauté for 2–3 minutes, until shallots soften and begin to turn translucent. Remove from heat and combine with the rice, apricots, dried cranberries, parsley, chives, garlic salt, and pepper. Stir well to incorporate.

Transfer rice mixture to a medium baking dish that you've coated with nonstick spray or brushed with olive oil. Cover and bake over indirect heat in the barbecue for 15–20 minutes, until top is browned. Serve hot.

SERVES 6-8

> 350°F
> indirect grilling

1 cup uncooked wild rice

3 cups low-sodium chicken or vegetable stock

¼ teaspoon seasoned salt

2–4 tablespoons butter

2 shallots, minced

1 garlic clove, crushed and minced

1 cup chopped dried apricots

1 cup dried sweetened cranberries

¼ cup chopped fresh parsley

⅛ cup finely chopped fresh chives

¼ teaspoon garlic salt

¼ teaspoon freshly ground black pepper

Biscuits and Gravy Stuffing

SERVES 8-10

425°F
direct grilling

8 cups chunks of breakfast biscuits (about the size of your thumbnail)

1 pound bulk breakfast sausage

1 cup butter, melted

¾ cup finely chopped onion

1½ cups finely chopped celery

½ cup diced apple, unpeeled

2 tablespoons extra-virgin olive oil

3 tablespoons cream

2 teaspoons ground sage

5 teaspoons poultry seasoning

¼ teaspoon freshly ground black pepper

The basis for this dish is that breakfast favorite — called "Sawmill Gravy" by some in the southern U.S. — that is traditionally served with buttermilk biscuits. If you want to make your own biscuits, I recommend the Jiffy brand (add a tablespoon of vegetable oil to the required water in the mix).

Put biscuit pieces into a large bowl and set aside.

In a medium skillet over hot grill, side burner, or stovetop, cook sausage, breaking it up with a fork, until done. Remove the sausage and pour drippings and scraped-up brown bits into a glass measuring cup. Add enough of the melted butter to make 1 full cup of liquid. Pour liquid into a bowl and set aside.

In another skillet, sauté the onion, celery, and apple in the olive oil over medium heat until the celery is just tender, but not browned. Pour the butter-drippings and cream into the skillet, stir, add the cooked sausage, and cook for 1 minute more. Carefully pour mixture over the biscuit pieces.

Add the ground sage, poultry seasoning, and pepper, and mix well. Cool, then use to stuff turkey.

Makes enough to stuff medium (12- to 14-pound) turkey.

Tequila Sweet Potatoes

If you don't wish to use tequila, you can substitute whiskey or bourbon for a smoky taste, coconut or pineapple rum for a sweet island tang, or Grand Marnier for an orange flavor.

Heat barbecue grill (or oven) to 350°F for grilling over direct heat.

Grate sweet potatoes or run them through a food processor using a grating disc. In a cast-iron skillet or Dutch oven over medium heat on barbecue grill, melt the butter, then add the olive oil. Add the grated potatoes and press them down with the back of a spoon into an even layer. Sprinkle with brown sugar and salt. Place the skillet in the barbecue and let cook in a covered grill for about an hour.

Add half of the tequila and half of the lime juice, stir, and press down again. Return to barbecue grill and continue cooking (covered) until the potatoes are tender and starting to brown around the edges, about another 20–25 minutes.

Remove and add the remaining tequila and lime juice. Stir and serve at the table directly from the hot cast-iron skillet.

SERVES 4-6

350°F
direct grilling

1 **pound sweet potatoes, peeled**

1 **cup butter**

2 **tablespoons extra-virgin olive oil**

6 **tablespoons brown sugar**

1 **teaspoon salt**

½ **cup tequila**

6 **tablespoons lime juice**

Savory Stuffed Potatoes

SERVES 6-8

350°F
direct grilling

---

12 small (2½- to 3-inch) red
   potatoes, skin on

6 garlic cloves, minced

¼ cup olive oil

2 tablespoons finely chopped
   basil leaves

½ teaspoon coarse salt

¼ teaspoon ground cumin

½ pound Huntsman cheese,
   grated

1 cup mayonnaise

2 tablespoons lemon juice

Freshly ground black pepper

Minced fresh chives for
   garnish

You can use your favorite strong cheese in this recipe, but the combination of Stilton and Double Gloucester in Huntsman cheese is incomparable in the stuffing both for flavor and texture.

In a medium pot, cook potatoes in salted water until water boils, then simmer them until they are tender, about 10–12 minutes longer. Drain potatoes, then plunge them into ice water, drain, and cool to room temperature, about 10 minutes.

In a skillet, cook the minced garlic in the olive oil until just starting to color. Remove pan from heat and drain garlic on paper towels. With a mortar and pestle, mash the garlic into a paste, place into a small bowl, then add the basil leaves, salt, and cumin; stir.

Preheat barbecue (or oven) to 350°F for grilling over direct heat.

Spoon the garlic-basil paste into a small bowl, and add the cheese, mayonnaise, and lemon juice. Sprinkle with freshly ground black pepper to taste.

Cut off the top half-inch of each cooled potato. Using a small melon-baller or a teaspoon, scoop out the inside of each potato, leaving a ¼-inch shell. Be very careful to not crush the thin sides. Chop the removed potato into small pieces and add to the bowl of garlic-basil paste; stir.

Using a small spoon, fill the potato skins with potato-garlic-basil mixture and put into a muffin pan, cut-side up. Place muffin pan on barbecue grill and cook in a covered grill until the cheese mixture is melted and bubbling, about 14–18 minutes.

Before serving, sprinkle tops of each potato with fresh chives for garnish.

Molasses New Potatoes

SERVES 4-6

350°F
direct grilling

¼ cup unsulphured molasses

3 tablespoons extra-virgin
olive oil

3 tablespoons very good-
quality balsamic vinegar

1 teaspoon dried thyme

1 teaspoon dried basil

1 teaspoon salt

3 pounds red potatoes,
unpeeled and cut into
quarters

½ cup coarsely chopped
pecans

¼ cup minced fresh chives
for garnish

If you wish you can substitute brown sugar, dark corn syrup, or pure maple syrup for the molasses, but the real thing gives a sweet, rich flavor that the other sweeteners just can't match. If you can find it, pomegranate molasses is wonderful in this dish. These potatoes are great with steak or roast beef.

Heat barbecue grill (or oven) to 350˚F for grilling over direct heat.

Butter a Dutch oven or a cast-iron skillet.

Warm the molasses by putting the open bottle in the microwave and heating on high for 10 seconds. In a small bowl, combine the warm molasses with the olive oil, vinegar, thyme, basil, and salt. Stir well.

Place potatoes in a resealable plastic bag and pour in the molasses mixture, rotating the bag to cover all the potatoes; let sit for 15 minutes. Pour the coated potatoes into the prepared Dutch oven or skillet, making sure all the liquid has been poured over the potatoes.

Bake in the barbecue, with lid closed, for about 20–25 minutes, then sprinkle on the pecans.

Continue cooking, stirring once or twice, for another 20 minutes or until the potatoes are tender and easily pierced with a fork.

Pour potatoes into a serving dish and garnish with the chives.

Cider Acorn Squash with Maple Syrup

*A*vailable year-round, acorn squash are in the "winter squash" family and are the most popular baking squash. They are available in gold and multicolored varieties as well as the signature green variety and can be stored for months in a cool basement or garage.

Heat barbecue grill (or oven) to 350°F for grilling over direct heat.

Spray a metal roasting pan or cast-iron skillet with cooking spray and fill with ¼-inch water.

Cut the squash in half lengthwise, perpendicular to the ribs. Scoop out the seeds with a sturdy spoon. Set the squash halves in the prepared baking pan and smear the flesh with the softened butter. Sprinkle the salt and pepper over each squash.

Pour ⅛ cup of cider into each squash half, then drizzle maple syrup over the cut edge of each squash so it drips down into the hollow. Mix cinnamon and cloves in a small dish, then sprinkle each half with the cinnamon-clove mixture.

Place the roasting pan or skillet in the center of the barbecue and roast the squash halves until nicely browned and fork-tender, about 45 minutes (depending on size of squash).

Remove the pan from the barbecue and, using a large spoon, remove the halves from the hot water. Sprinkle squash with brown sugar and serve warm.

SERVES 4

350°F
direct grilling

- 2 acorn squash
- 3 tablespoons unsalted butter, softened
- ½ teaspoon kosher salt
- Ground black pepper
- ½ cup apple cider
- 4 tablespoons pure maple syrup
- 1 teaspoon ground cinnamon
- ¼ teaspoon ground cloves
- Sprinkle of brown sugar, for serving

Herbed Spaghetti Squash

350°F
indirect grilling

1 (3-pound) spaghetti squash

1 tablespoon butter

½ teaspoon brown sugar

1 tablespoon minced fresh
  parsley

½ teaspoon dried savory

¼ teaspoon dried oregano

¼ teaspoon salt

⅛ teaspoon black pepper

Dash of dried whole sage,
  crushed

Fresh rosemary for garnish

This type of squash is a delight to cook and is a refreshing change from other types of squash. By using some spaghetti sauce you can even get your kids to like it. The larger the vegetable, the thicker the strands and the more flavorful the taste. Spaghetti squash can be baked, boiled, or steamed.

Heat barbecue grill (or oven) to 350°F for grilling over indirect heat.

Wash squash and cut in half lengthwise. With a large spoon, remove and discard the seeds. Place the squash halves, cut-side down, in a baking pan or Dutch oven and add water so that it covers 2½ inches of the squash. Place the pan in the barbecue grill, close lid of grill, and bring the water to a boil. Cover the pan, move it to the unheated side of the grill, and cook, covered, for an additional 20–25 minutes, or until the squash is fork-tender inside.

Drain the squash and cool. Using a fork, remove the spaghetti-like squash strands and discard the empty shells. Place the squash into a serving bowl, and add the butter, brown sugar, parsley, savory, oregano, salt and pepper, and crushed sage. Toss gently.

Garnish with a sprinkle of fresh rosemary leaves.

Sautéed Citrus Beets

SERVES 4-6

350°F
direct/indirect grilling

*W*hen cooking beets, especially in water, leave the skin on while cooking, which minimizes leaking of the strong purple pigment and loss of nutrients from the roots. Despite being the veggie with the highest sugar content (ever heard of sugar beets?), they are low in calories.

Heat barbecue grill (or oven) to 350°F for grilling over direct and indirect heat.

In a large saucepan or skillet on the grill or side burner, sauté the onion slices in butter until tender, then add the cornstarch and stir well. Add the zests, citrus juices, currant jelly, salt, and pepper, and stir gently. Bring to a boil for 2 minutes, stirring constantly.

Add the beets, folding them into the liquid. Move the pan to the indirect heating side of the grill. Close the lid and cook until beets are hot, approximately 10 minutes. Remove from grill and transfer to a warmed bowl. Sprinkle with parsley and serve.

1 small onion, cut in ¼-inch slices

2 tablespoons butter

2 tablespoons cornstarch

1 teaspoon grated orange zest

1 teaspoon grated lemon zest

1 cup orange juice

2 tablespoons lemon juice

¼ cup currant jelly, melted

¼ teaspoon salt

¼ teaspoon white pepper

1 (16-ounce) can sliced beets, drained

Fresh parsley for garnish

Pumpkin and Butternut Squash Pie

400°/350°F
indirect grilling

1 (9-inch) pie crust, unbaked

1½ cups cooked and mashed sugar pumpkin flesh, cooled (or solid-pack canned pumpkin)

1½ cups cooked and mashed butternut squash, cooled

1 (12-ounce) can evaporated milk

½ cup cream

¾ cup packed light brown sugar

1½ teaspoons ground cinnamon

¼ teaspoon ground nutmeg

⅛ teaspoon ground cloves

½ teaspoon ground ginger

4 large eggs

1 tablespoon dark rum

Whipping or heavy cream, whipped

For the best results, don't use regular pumpkins; they often produce a stringy and bland filling. Instead, select smaller "sugar" or "pie" pumpkins as they have more meat inside and offer the best texture and flavor.

Heat barbecue grill (or oven) to 400°F for grilling over indirect heat.

Line pie crust with foil and fill with pie weights, uncooked rice, or dry beans. Bake the crust for 15 minutes on the heated side of the covered grill. Carefully remove the foil and pie weights, prick bottom of pie with a fork several times, and bake 5 minutes longer or until golden. Cool the pie crust on a wire rack.

Open vents to cool the barbecue to 350°F.

In large bowl, whisk together the pumpkin, squash, evaporated milk, cream, sugar, cinnamon, nutmeg, cloves, ginger, eggs, and rum. Pour the pumpkin-squash mixture into the cooled pie crust. Cover the edge of the crust with pieces of aluminum foil to prevent burning.

Bake the pie over indirect heat in the covered barbecue for 60–70 minutes or until a knife inserted in the center of the pie comes out clean.

Cool pie on wire rack for 1–1½ hours, then cover and refrigerate until chilled.

To serve, pipe with whipped cream or serve whipped cream separately.

Sour Cream Raisin Pie

If you don't have sour cream, here is a quick and tasty substitute. Mix ¼ cup skim milk, 1 cup dry-curd cottage cheese, and 2 tablespoons lemon juice in a blender. Blend until smooth, then add 1 teaspoon salt and blend for 30 seconds.

Heat barbecue grill (or oven) to 350°F for grilling over indirect heat.

Combine raisins, sour cream, buttermilk, cornstarch, salt, brown sugar, cinnamon, nutmeg, and lemon zest in a large saucepan over medium heat. Stir until well blended, then bring to a boil. Continue to cook while stirring constantly, until the mixture becomes thick. Remove from heat.

Beat the 3 egg yolks and half-and-half together. Add 3 tablespoons of the hot mixture to the egg mixture and stir, then fold the egg mixture into the hot raisin mixture, stirring briskly. Return to the heat and cook until thickened, stirring constantly, for about 2 minutes. Remove from the heat and pour into the pie shell.

For the meringue, beat the 3 egg whites until frothy, gradually adding the sugar and continuing to beat until stiff peaks form. Add vanilla and stir. Add the meringue to the pie, spreading it from edge to edge, covering the whole pie.

Place the pie in the barbecue over indirect heat, close the lid, and cook for 10-15 minutes, peeking several times. Remove the pie when the meringue peaks have just turned golden brown.

SERVES 6-8

350°F
indirect grilling

1 cup golden raisins

1 cup dark raisins

¾ cup sour cream

¾ cup buttermilk

3 tablespoons cornstarch

¾ teaspoon salt

¾ cup brown sugar

1 teaspoon ground cinnamon

¾ teaspoon ground nutmeg

1 teaspoon freshly grated lemon zest

3 eggs, separated

½ cup half-and-half

1 9-inch baked pastry shell

Meringue:

3 egg whites (from above)

6 tablespoons white sugar

½ teaspoon vanilla extract

Cranberry and Grand Marnier Tart Tatin

> 350°F
> indirect grilling

Topping:

⅓ cup unsalted butter

⅔ cup packed light brown
  sugar

2 cups fresh cranberries

½ cup golden raisins

Batter:

1½ cups all-purpose flour

2 teaspoons baking powder

¼ teaspoon ground nutmeg

3 tablespoons finely grated
  orange zest

¼ teaspoon salt

8 tablespoons (1 stick)
  softened unsalted butter

1 cup granulated sugar

3 tablespoons Grand Marnier
  (optional)

2 large eggs, separated

½ cup whole milk

¼ teaspoon cream of tartar

2 cups whipped cream,
  flavored with 1 tablespoon
  Grand Marnier

Cranberries are very important crops in certain parts of the U.S. They are most often used in juices, jellies or sauces, and in a dried-sweetened form. But fresh cranberries have a richness that is absent in these other forms, but they certainly can be sour! The brown sugar and golden raisins used in this tart offset the inherent acidic bitterness of the fresh fruit.

Heat barbecue grill (or oven) to 350°F for grilling over indirect heat.

Heavily spray a 9- or 10-inch cast-iron Dutch oven with a nonstick cooking spray, or butter the pan generously.

In a small saucepan over medium heat, combine the butter and brown sugar, stirring and cooking until the butter melts and the sugar has dissolved. Continue heating for a few more minutes until the sugar starts to caramelize and to turn light brown. Remove the pan from the heat, and pour the hot liquid into the bottom of your prepared Dutch oven. Sprinkle the syrup generously with fresh cranberries and raisins, completely covering the bottom of the Dutch oven.

In a large mixing bowl, whisk together the flour, baking powder, nutmeg, 2 tablespoons of the orange zest, and salt.

With an electric mixer, cream the butter with the sugar until it becomes light and fluffy, about 3 minutes. Using a rubber spatula, scrape down the sides of the bowl and then add 1 tablespoon of the liqueur (if using), and the egg yolks, one at a time, beating well after each step.

Once again scrape the sides of the bowl, then add a third of the flour mixture. Add half of the milk, then add another third of the flour, second half of milk, and then final third of flour, beating well after each addition.

In a medium bowl, whisk the egg whites with the cream of tartar until the whites form stiff peaks.

With a large spatula, gently fold half of the beaten egg whites into the cake batter. Then add second half of the beaten whites, again folding in gently. Fold in the remaining 2 tablespoons Grand Marnier.

Pour the batter into the Dutch oven over the cranberries, smoothing the top with the spatula. Bake over indirect heat for 25–35 minutes in a covered grill, rotating once during the cooking time. Check to make sure the top has browned nicely and has begun to separate from the sides of the Dutch oven. Remove the cake from the barbecue and place on a wire rack to cool for about 10–15 minutes.

To remove the cake, run a sharp knife around the sides of the Dutch oven to loosen it completely. Place a serving plate face-down over the Dutch oven, and then quickly turn the pan over to transfer the cake onto the serving plate. Cool to room temperature.

Serve with flavored whipped cream, lightly sprinkled with the remaining orange zest.

Sue's Apple Crisp with a Twist

SERVES 8-10

> 350°F
> direct grilling

6-8 cups peeled and sliced apples (about 12 medium apples)

¼ cup lemon juice

1 tablespoon lemon zest

1 cup sugar (or to taste, depending on the type of apple)

½ cup golden raisins

Topping:

1½ cups brown sugar

1½ cups rolled oats

1¼ cups all-purpose flour

Pinch of salt

12 tablespoons (1½ sticks) softened butter

2 tablespoons grated lemon zest

1½ tablespoons ground cinnamon

½ tablespoon ground nutmeg

1 tablespoon ground cardamom (optional)

1 cup chopped nuts

Ice cream or whipped cream, for serving

Twist of lemon and fresh mint to garnish

In 2008, I judged a campground barbecue contest in Calhous Falls, South Carolina, and Sue Hannah's apple crisp entry dazzled the judges with its simplicity, flavor, and wonderful texture. This was probably the best apple crisp I've ever enjoyed.

Heat barbecue grill (or oven) to 350°F for grilling over direct heat.

In a large bowl, mix the apples, lemon juice, lemon zest, sugar, and raisins. Stir to mix thoroughly. Spread the apple mixture into the bottom of a sprayed or buttered 12-inch Dutch oven or cast-iron skillet.

In a medium bowl, mix the brown sugar, oats, flour, salt, butter, lemon zest, cinnamon, nutmeg, cardamom, and chopped nuts. Mix well, then pour it over the apples in the Dutch oven or skillet.

Bake in the center of the covered barbecue for 25–30 minutes. Continue baking until the apples are cooked and the topping is brown.

Serve warm with ice cream or whipped cream. Garnish with a twist of lemon and mint.

Grilled Pears with Cinnamon and Maple Syrup

I'm fortunate to live in "pear heaven," the state of Washington, just across the Columbia River from Oregon, which many say are the best two states in the country for growing pears. I prefer the Bartlett variety, but the Comice and Seckel varieties are just as wonderful in this recipe. You can serve a big dollop of fresh whipped cream or French vanilla ice cream alongside the fruit for a decadent dessert.

Heat barbecue grill (or oven) to 350°F for grilling over direct heat.

Place the butter, apple juice, syrup, cinnamon, ginger, and cloves in a small saucepan. Simmer on side burner or stovetop until the butter and maple syrup have melted together, stir well, remove from heat, and keep warm.

Peel and core the pears from the bottom, making sure you don't go up into the neck of the fruit. Leave the stems on. (If you are preparing a large number of pears, brush them with lemon juice to keep the fruit from turning brown.)

Stand the pears upright in a cast-iron skillet or Dutch oven with the vegetable oil, and set the skillet on the grill over indirect heat. Cook for 15–20 minutes, covered, basting the fruit with the spiced syrup several times as the pears cook.

Remove the fruit from the heat, let cool slightly (they should be warm, not hot), and serve with a final spoonful of glaze drizzled over each pear.

SERVES 6

350°F
direct grilling

Glaze:

3 tablespoons unsalted butter

¼ cup apple juice

¼ cup good-quality maple syrup

½ teaspoon ground cinnamon

¼ teaspoon ground ginger

⅛ teaspoon ground cloves

6 pears (your favorite variety)

3 tablespoons vegetable oil

Winter Recipes

MENU ONE:

Herb-Crusted Prime Rib Roast (124)
Mrs. Petersen's Yorkshire Pudding (142)
Orange and White Au Gratins (146)
Granny Kate's Korn Puddin' (150)
Hausfrau's German Chocolate Soufflé (155)

MENU TWO:

Barbecue Crown Roast of Pork (128)
Savory Seasonal Skillet Stuffing (138)
Parmigiano-Reggiano-Shallot Risotto (148)
Skillet-Grilled Root Vegetables (152)
Tricia's Barbecue Bread Pudding (154)

A LA CARTE WINTER RECIPES:

Beef Tenderloin with Pinot-
   Mushroom Sauce (126)
Tennessee Smoked Ham (127)
Grilled Goose with Apple-
   Apricot-Prune Stuffing (129)
Carolina-Style Pork
   Shoulder (130)
Grilled Leg of Lamb with
   Pomegranate Sauce (132)
Grill-Baked Oysters (134)
Grilled Pacific Salmon (135)
Herb Focaccia Bread (136)

Parker House Onion Rolls (137)
Rustic Garlic-Mashed
   Potatoes (144)
White and Gold Potato
   Patties (145)
Hawaiian Sweet Potatoes (147)
Creamed Peas with Mint (149)
Honey-Butter Brussels
   Sprouts (151)
SixNine Pecan Pie (153)
Eggnog Popovers (156)
Mrs. Browne's Butter Tarts (157)

Herb-Crusted Prime Rib Roast

SERVES 6-8

350°F
direct grilling

---

1 (5- to 6-pound) 3- or 4-rib prime rib roast, trimmed, chine bone removed

4 tablespoons extra-virgin olive oil

1 tablespoon salt

1 tablespoon dried rosemary

1 tablespoon dried savory

½ teaspoon freshly ground black pepper

½ teaspoon fresh lemon juice

1 teaspoon grated lemon zest

1½ cups fresh breadcrumbs

½ cup chopped fresh parsley

1 tablespoon granulated garlic

¼ cup prepared yellow mustard

Fresh rosemary sprigs for garnish

Restaurant note: I don't recommend restaurants in this book, but if you are ever in London, do not miss a visit to Roast. It's located in the Floral Hall on Stoney Street, a historic part of London, and surely the gateway to roast beef heaven. Just the name from the menu — Roast Rib of Welsh Black Beef with Yorkshire Pudding, Creamed Horseradish and Mustard — causes a shiver up my culinary spine.

Heat barbecue grill (or oven) to 350°F for grilling over direct heat.

In a medium roasting pan, place rib roast, fat-side up. Brush all surfaces with 3 tablespoons of olive oil and then rub all over with salt, dried rosemary, savory, and pepper. Put roast into the barbecue and close lid.

In a small bowl, mix the lemon juice and zest, breadcrumbs, parsley, remaining 1 tablespoon olive oil, and garlic. Set aside.

After the prime rib has roasted 1½ hours, remove it from the barbecue and roasting pan. Generously brush the mustard over the entire roast, then gently press the breadcrumb mixture onto the mustard-coated roast.

Place the roast back in the pan and the barbecue. Cook for 1 hour longer or until the coating is golden and a meat thermometer inserted into the center of roast, not touching a bone, registers 135°F.

Remove the pan from the grill, place the meat on a heated platter, cover with aluminum foil, and let it rest for 10 minutes to let the juices redistribute throughout the roast. The internal temperature of meat will rise to 145°F (medium-rare) upon standing.

Use the remaining drippings in the pan to make Yorkshire pudding or gravy, or brush the fat on a pan of roasted potatoes 10 minutes before taking them out of the oven.

Garnish roast with rosemary sprigs and slice at the table. For a perfect dinner, accompany the roast prime rib with Yorkshire pudding (see recipe on page 142).

Beef Tenderloin with Pinot-Mushroom Sauce

SERVES 6-8

500°F
direct grilling

½ ounce each dried morel,
   shitakes, and chanterelles

1½ cups hot water

½ teaspoon garlic salt

½ teaspoon freshly ground
   black pepper

½ teaspoon ground ginger

¼ teaspoon ground coriander

¼ teaspoon ground cumin

4 tablespoons extra-virgin
   olive oil

1 (3- to 4-pound) beef
   tenderloin, cut from the
   wider loin end

1 cup minced shallots (about
   ¼ pound)

4 tablespoons (½ stick) cold
   butter

2 tablespoons red wine vinegar

2 tablespoons balsamic
   vinegar

1 cup favorite Pinot Noir
   wine

1 (14-ounce) can low-sodium
   beef broth (I like Swanson's)

Salt and pepper to taste

Freshly chopped parsley for
   garnish

If you'd rather cook the tenderloin as steaks, you merely need to sear them over high heat for about 1 minute per side, then over indirect heat for 2–3 minutes per side. As with the roast, when the internal temperature reaches 135˚F, remove from grill, cover, and let rest 10 minutes to recirculate juices.

Heat barbecue grill (or oven) to 500˚F for grilling over direct heat.

In a medium bowl, rehydrate the mushrooms in the hot water for a minimum of 20 minutes. Strain the mushrooms and reserve the liquid. Mince the mushrooms and set aside.

Mix garlic salt, pepper, ginger, coriander, and cumin in a small bowl.

Massage 3 tablespoons of the olive oil into the meat, sprinkle on the spice mixture and pat into all sides, including the ends of the meat (do not rub).

Place the meat on a rack in a roasting pan and cook in the covered barbecue for 25–30 minutes, or until a meat thermometer registers 135˚F for a medium-rare roast.

While the meat is cooking, sauté the shallots in a small skillet with 1 tablespoon each of the butter, the red wine vinegar, and remaining olive oil over low heat. Cook, stirring, until the shallots are wilted and soft. Add the balsamic vinegar, and boil the mixture until the liquid is almost evaporated, about 3 minutes. Add the minced mushrooms, their soaking liquid, the wine, and the beef broth. Boil the mixture, then turn down to simmer, and cook until the sauce is reduced by half, about 2 cups. Add the salt and pepper to taste.

When the meat is medium-rare, remove it from the heat and transfer to a heated platter. Cover loosely with foil and let it stand for 15–20 minutes. Its temperature will rise to 145˚F while it rests.

Whisk the pan juices into the reduced sauce and swirl in the remaining 3 tablespoons butter, whisking until it's fully incorporated. Transfer the sauce to a heated sauceboat.

Slice the tenderloin in 1-inch-thick slices and serve with a tablespoon of the mushroom sauce on each slice, sprinkled with freshly chopped parsley.

Tennessee Smoked Ham

This recipe was adapted from one shared with me during one of my many visits to the Memphis in May barbecue festival. The head chef of the Airpork Crew and I sat around talking about regional recipes, and we came up with this as a perfect example of an ideal ham recipe.

Soak a handful of wood chips (hickory, pecan, or cherry) in water for at least ½ hour before you are ready to grill.

Heat barbecue grill (or oven) to 350°F for grilling over indirect heat, with water pan under unheated side.

Prepare a smoke package by placing a handful of presoaked wood chips onto a 12-inch-square of aluminum foil. Then fold the foil over to make an envelope, sealing in the chips. Punch 2–3 holes in top of the package, being careful not to go through the bottom. Place packet directly on hot coals or gas flame.

Score the ham fat a dozen or so times in a diamond pattern to allow the sauce to seep into the meat.

In a medium saucepan over high heat, combine all the remaining ingredients except the fresh parsley. Bring the sauce to a full boil, then reduce the heat to low and simmer, uncovered, for 14 minutes, stirring often. Remove from the heat, divide into 4 portions in small bowls, and set aside.

Place the wood chip packet on the coals or the gas flame, then place the ham on the heated side of grill, brush with one portion of the sauce, close barbecue lid, and cook for 20 minutes, turning twice.

Remove the ham from the direct heat and place on the grill over the water pan. Generously brush the ham with the second portion of sauce. Close the barbecue and grill for 2–2½ hours, until a meat thermometer inserted into the meat registers 140–150°F. During cooking, baste 2 or 3 times with the third portion of the sauce.

When cooked, remove the ham from the grill, cover with aluminum foil, and let it rest for 15 minutes before slicing.

Warm the remaining sauce, sprinkle it with chopped parsley, and serve in a heated sauceboat alongside the sliced ham.

SERVES 10-12

350°F
indirect grilling
water pan
wood chips

1 (6- to 7-pound) bone-in ham, cooked

1 cup ketchup

⅓ cup finely chopped onion

⅓ cup pure maple syrup

⅓ cup orange marmalade

⅓ cup cider vinegar

¼ cup ginger ale

2 tablespoons lemon juice

3 tablespoons yellow mustard

1 teaspoon dried oregano

1 teaspoon garlic granules

1 teaspoon ground cumin

1 teaspoon dried marjoram

⅛ teaspoon ground cloves

1 teaspoon minced fresh garlic

1 teaspoon dried sweet red pepper flakes

2 tablespoons chopped fresh parsley, to serve

Barbecue Crown Roast of Pork

> 500°F
> indirect grilling
> wood chips
> spray bottle

1 (7- to 8-pound) crown roast
of pork (two racks tied in
a circle)

10 garlic cloves, sliced thin

Rub:

2 tablespoons chopped fresh
rosemary

1 tablespoon chopped fresh
sage

1 tablespoon kosher salt

1 teaspoon lemon pepper

Spray:

1 cup apple juice

2 tablespoons extra-virgin
olive oil

1 teaspoon balsamic vinegar

The bones should be "Frenched," by cutting the meat and fat away from each end of the rib down about 2–3 inches from the end. Also use small pieces of foil to cover the bare bones on the crown so they don't burn. Remove foil before serving.

Insert a sharp knife ½-inch into the roast on all sides. Slip the garlic slices into these pockets. Combine the rosemary, sage, salt, and pepper, and stir. Spread the rub all over the roast and into the crevices. Let stand at room temperature 1 hour before grilling.

Soak a handful of wood chips (hickory, pecan, or cherry) in water for at least ½ hour before you are ready to grill.

Heat barbecue grill (or oven) to 500°F for grilling over indirect heat, placing a water pan under unheated side.

Prepare a smoke package by placing a handful of presoaked wood chips onto a 12-inch-square of aluminum foil. Then fold the foil over to make an envelope, sealing in the chips. Punch 2–3 holes in top of the package, being careful not to go through the bottom. Place package directly on hot coals or gas flame.

In a spray bottle, combine apple juice, olive oil, and vinegar. Set aside.

Cook the roast in covered barbecue over direct heat for 30 minutes, turning several times to sear all over.

After 30 minutes, move the roast to the unheated side of the grill over a water pan. Cook, with grill covered, until the internal temperature reaches 145°F, about 2½–3 hours longer. Spray the roast with the apple spray 2 or 3 times while it cooks.

Remove the roast from the grill, spray once more, then lightly cover with foil. Let the roast rest 20 minutes before carving. Cut and remove the string from the roast and slice between the rib bones. Serve one rib section with bone per person.

Grilled Goose with Apple-Apricot-Prune Stuffing

When cooking a domestic goose, it's important to prick the skin, especially on the legs and wings. Geese have more fat than turkeys or chickens and the holes help to let the fat drip out when it's cooking.

Heat barbecue grill (or oven) to 350°F for indirect heating, placing water pan under unheated side. Place the dried apricots in a bowl containing 2 cups of hot water and re-hydrate for 20 minutes.

Clean the goose, removing excess fat inside cavity, then rinse the goose well and pat completely dry. Spray the goose with nonstick cooking spray, then sprinkle the skin with salt, and the cavity of the bird with poultry seasoning. Prick the skin all over with a fork, then place the bird in a roasting pan, breast up. Put the roasting pan in the barbecue, over the water pan. Close grill.

Grill 2½–3 hours or until the goose is tender, the juices from a knife inserted into the thigh run clear, and the temperature on a meat thermometer inserted into the thigh reaches 180°F. To brown and crisp-up the skin, move the roasting pan to the heated side of the grill for the last 15–20 minutes of cooking.

While the goose is cooking, place the prunes and ¼ cup white wine in a large bowl. Soak for 10 minutes, add the apples, the drained apricots, the crumbled bread, raisins, lime juice, sugar, salt, nutmeg, and cinnamon. Stir to mix well. Place in a loaf pan, which you've sprayed with nonstick spray or brushed with olive oil, and tightly cover with aluminum foil.

Place the pan of stuffing on the unheated side of the grill for the last hour of the goose cooking time. Remove foil for last 15 minutes to crisp up the top of the stuffing.

Remove the roasting pan from the barbecue grill. Place the cooked goose on a heated platter, cover with foil, and let rest for 15 minutes to make carving easier. Reserve the fat in the pan for gravy.

In a saucepan, heat the remaining ¾ cup wine, ¼ cup water, 4 tablespoons of drippings from the roasting pan, and several tablespoons of the stuffing (to thicken the gravy). Bring the mixture to a boil, stirring often, and then simmer for 5 minutes. Serve the gravy in a sauceboat (some like to strain it; I like the chunks). Season with salt and freshly ground black pepper, and sprinkle with paprika before serving.

SERVES 4-6

350°F
indirect grilling
water pan

½ cup diced dried apricots

1 (7- to 8-pound) frozen domestic goose, thawed

2 tablespoons kosher salt

2 teaspoons poultry seasoning

1 cup pitted and diced prunes

1 cup white wine

2 cups diced red apple, unpeeled

4 slices stale rye bread, finely crumbled

3 tablespoons golden raisins

1 tablespoon fresh lime juice

1 teaspoon brown sugar

½ teaspoon salt

⅓ teaspoon ground nutmeg

⅓ teaspoon ground cinnamon

Salt and freshly ground pepper to taste

Paprika for garnish

Carolina-Style Pork Shoulder

SERVES 10-12

350°F
indirect grilling
water pan
wood chips
season 3–24 hours

Rub:

2 tablespoons salt

2 tablespoons brown sugar

1 teaspoon ground cumin

2 tablespoons paprika

1 tablespoon granulated garlic

1 tablespoon citrus black pepper

2 teaspoons paprika

1 (6- to 7-pound) bone-in pork butt (shoulder)

Basting sauce:

½ cup bourbon

2 tablespoons molasses

½ cup balsamic vinegar

1½ cups apple juice

2 tablespoons salt

1 tablespoon crushed red pepper flakes

1 tablespoon freshly ground black pepper

1 tablespoon granulated garlic

Carolina barbecue sauces feature vinegar, red pepper, sugar, and sometimes molasses or Worcestershire sauce. The Carolinas eschew tomatoes in most everything except BLTs. Also, the style of pulling, shredding, or chopping is very popular in both the Carolinas. The meat is sliced, chopped, or can be pulled into strands, drizzled with sauce, and either served in a bun (sometimes with cole-slaw on top of the meat) or on a plate with side dishes like beans, potato salad, hush puppies, or grilled vegetables.

Mix the rub ingredients in a medium bowl. Rub the pork shoulder on all surfaces with the mixture, cover, and refrigerate from 3 hours or up to 24 hours.

Soak a handful of wood chips (hickory, pecan, or cherry) in water for at least ½ hour before you are ready to grill.

Heat barbecue grill (or oven) to 350°F for grilling over indirect heat, placing a water pan under the unheated side of the grill.

Mix the ingredients for the basting sauce in a small saucepan.

Prepare a smoke package by placing a handful of presoaked wood chips onto a 12-inch-square of aluminum foil. Then fold the foil over to make an envelope, sealing in the chips. Punch 2–3 holes in top of the package, being careful not to go through the bottom. Place packet directly on hot coals or gas flame.

Smoke the pork shoulder over indirect heat over a water pan, adding more charcoal, or managing gas flame to maintain a medium-low heat of between 270°F to 320°F. Smoke/grill until the internal temperature of the shoulder is 145°F, about 3–4 hours. During the cooking time you can sprinkle wood chips on the coals or flames several times to give the meat a nice smoky flavor.

During the last couple of hours of cooking, baste the shoulder quickly every 30 minutes, remembering you can lose 15 minutes of cooking time each time you open the lid of the smoker. Boil any leftover basting sauce for 10 minutes, then cool.

When pork is cooked, remove from grill and slice, pull, or chop the pork, add sauce, and stir it into the meat before serving as noted at top of recipe.

Grilled Leg of Lamb with Pomegranate Sauce

SERVES 6-8

350°F
direct grilling
marinate 2–3 days

1 (5- to 6-pound) leg of lamb

Marinade:

3 whole Spanish onions,
   thinly sliced

1 quart pomegranate juice
   (available in health food
   section of most markets)

4 cloves garlic, chopped

1 cup extra-virgin olive oil

Juice of 2 lemons

2 teaspoons fresh rosemary,
   or 1 tablespoon dried
   rosemary

1 teaspoon dried marjoram

1 teaspoon dried oregano

1 teaspoon dried summer
   savory

1 teaspoon coarsely ground
   black pepper

2 teaspoons coarse sea salt

Pomegranate sauce:

2 tablespoons butter

1 tablespoon brown sugar

1 tablespoon fresh rosemary,
   or ½ tablespoon dried

Seeds of 1 medium
   pomegranate

One of the keys to this recipe is a long marinating period. I usually marinate the lamb for 2 to 3 days! Always marinate the meat in the refrigerator, and I try to turn it over 2 or 3 times a day.

Have the butcher butterfly the leg of lamb, or do it yourself.

Combine all marinade ingredients in a large bowl and whisk until completely mixed. Pour marinade into a large plastic bag (a garbage bag does fine), and put this inside a similar bag. Add the lamb, turning to make sure it is coated on all sides.

Marinate for TWO to THREE DAYS in refrigerator. No kidding, 2–3 days! It's well worth the wait. Turn bag over 2–3 times a day.

Heat grill to 350°F for grilling over direct heat.

Drain the leg of lamb, reserving the marinade. Strain the marinade into a saucepan and boil for at least 12 minutes. Cool, set aside half of the liquid to baste the meat while cooking, and leave the other half in the saucepan as a base for the pomegranate sauce.

Place lamb on grill for 12–15 minutes on each side, brushing occasionally with the marinade. Internal temperature should be 125°F to 130°F.

To make the pomegranate sauce, begin with the boiled marinade already in the saucepan. Add butter, brown sugar, and rosemary. Heat, stirring, until thoroughly mixed and the sugar has dissolved. Just before removing the sauce from heat, add the pomegranate seeds, and stir quickly. Remove the pan from heat and pour the warm sauce into a serving dish to pass at the table.

Remove meat from the barbecue, cover, and let rest 5 minutes. Slice the meat and serve with the warm pomegranate sauce.

Grill-Baked Oysters

> 325°F
> direct grilling

1 teaspoon salt

½ teaspoon cayenne pepper

2 tablespoons fines herbes

½ teaspoon granulated garlic

8 tablespoons (1 stick)
melted butter

4 cups cubed Italian or
French bread (½-inch cubes)

1 pint raw oysters, well-
drained

1 tablespoon grated lemon
zest

1 tablespoon lemon juice

1 small onion, minced

3 tablespoons minced chives

⅔ cup heavy cream or half-
and-half

¼ cup freshly minced parsley
for garnish

1 tablespoon Hungarian
paprika for garnish

Serve these luscious grill-baked oysters with thick slices of toasted and buttered sourdough garlic bread, and chilled glasses of fruity white wine like a Gewürztraminer or young Riesling.

Heat barbecue grill (or oven) to 325˚F for grilling over direct heat.

Mix salt, cayenne, fines herbes, and garlic in a small bowl.

Pour half the melted butter (¼ cup) into a cast-iron skillet, add half of the bread cubes, and then cook over indirect heat until they're golden-brown. Lightly sprinkle the bread with some of the herb-spice mix, stir quickly, remove from the pan, and set aside.

Pour the remaining melted butter into the pan and fry the rest of the cubes until brown, then sprinkle with the herb-spice mix. Remove the pan from the grill and top the bread cubes in it with half of the oysters and sprinkle with half of each of the minced lemon zest, lemon juice, onion, and chives.

Cover the oysters with half of the remaining bread cubes, then sprinkle with the remaining lemon zest, lemon juice, onion, and chives. Cover with the remaining oysters.

Top the oysters with the last quarter of the bread cubes, pour the cream over the bread and oysters, and bake in the covered barbecue for 20–30 minutes.

Remove the pan from the barbecue, sprinkle with freshly chopped parsley and paprika as a garnish, and serve.

Grilled Pacific Salmon

There are four main kinds of Pacific salmon: Chinook or King, Sockeye or Red, Coho or Silver, and the priciest of all, Copper River Salmon. Chinooks are the largest and considered the tastiest — that is, except for the gourmet Copper River variety, which is available only 4 to 5 weeks a year in May through June. This smoked salmon is delicious with grilled vegetables and rice pilaf, wild rice, or fragrant jasmine rice.

Bone the fillet using tweezers or needle-nose pliers. Do not remove the skin. Place in a glass or stainless steel pan.

Combine all ingredients for the first rub, mix well, and pack onto the flesh side of the fillet. DO NOT RUB IN. Cover the fillet with plastic wrap, refrigerate, and let rest for 3 hours to allow the rub to draw out liquid from the fillet. Rinse the fillet in cool clean water to remove the dry rub and pat dry. Allow to dry for about 30 minutes, until the flesh becomes tacky.

Soak a handful of wood chips (alder, pecan, or cherry) in water for at least ½ hour before you are ready to grill.

Prepare grill for direct heating at 350°F.

To add smoke flavor to the grilled fish: If using a charcoal grill, sprinkle presoaked wood chips on coals just before you put the fish on the grill. If using a gas grill, make a smoke package by putting a handful of presoaked wood chips on a 12-inch-square sheet of aluminum foil, fold over the foil to form an envelope, and puncture the top of the foil with a pencil 2–3 times (do not go through the bottom). Place the packet on the gas flame.

Combine all the ingredients for the finishing rub and sprinkle it on the fillet (it will be thick — about twice the amount you would use if you were heavily salting and peppering). Place the fillet on a piece of heavy-duty aluminum foil that you have sprayed with cooking oil.

Cook with the lid closed until the temperature in the thickest part of the fillet reaches 155°F (about 10 minutes). Let rest for 5 minutes and then serve.

SERVES 4-6

350°F
direct grilling
wood chips
season 3+ hours

3-pound fresh fillet of wild salmon, skin left on

First rub:
1 cup light brown sugar
½ cup salt
6 tablespoons garlic salt
6 tablespoons onion salt
1 tablespoon dried dill weed
1 tablespoon dried summer savory
2 teaspoons dried tarragon

Finishing rub:
¼ cup light brown sugar
1 tablespoon granulated garlic
1 tablespoon granulated onion
1 teaspoon dried summer savory
1 teaspoon dried tarragon

Herb Focaccia Bread

> 450°F
> indirect grilling

2¾ cups all-purpose
unbleached flour

1 teaspoon salt

1 teaspoon sugar

1 tablespoon active dry yeast

1 teaspoon garlic powder

1 teaspoon dried oregano

1 teaspoon dried thyme

1 teaspoon dried rosemary
leaves, crushed

½ teaspoon dried basil

1 pinch freshly ground black
pepper

3 tablespoons olive oil

1 cup water

1 tablespoon freshly grated
Parmesan cheese

First baked in Rome as (love this name) panis focacius, focaccia is an oven-baked flat bread that is very popular in Italy, Greece, France, Spain, and through-out the Mediterranean. The main ingredients include olive oil, herbs, cheese, and sometimes meat and garden vegetables.

Heat barbecue grill (or oven) to 450°F for grilling over indirect heat.

In a large bowl, stir together the flour, salt, sugar, yeast, garlic powder, oregano, thyme, rosemary, basil, and black pepper. Mix in 1 tablespoon of the olive oil and the cup of water. Continue stirring until the dough has pulled together. Scrape the sides of the bowl and turn the dough out onto a lightly floured surface; knead until smooth and elastic.

Lightly oil a large bowl, place the dough in the bowl, and turn to coat with oil. Cover with a damp cloth, and let rise in a warm place (a slightly warm oven with the door open) for 20 minutes (see "warm place" ideas on opposite page).

Punch the dough down and then place it on a greased (or sprayed with nonstick spray) baking sheet with a rim (such as a jelly-roll pan). Using your fingers, stretch and pat the dough into a ½-inch-thick rectangle. Brush the top with the remaining 2 tablespoons olive oil, and then sprinkle with the grated Parmesan cheese.

Bake, covered, on the unheated side of the preheated barbecue for 15 minutes, or until golden brown. Serve warm.

Parker House Onion Rolls

If you ever have trouble finding a warm place to let yeast dough rise, try turning on an oven to 200°F for 10 minutes, then turn it off and put bowl inside the oven and leave the door open. Or place a large, shallow pan on the lowest shelf in an unlit oven and pour in 2 inches of boiling water. Place the covered dough on the rack above the hot water, and close the oven door.

In a small saucepan, warm the milk over low heat (between 110°F and 115°F). Then pour ⅓ cup of the milk into a small bowl, add the yeast, and let it sit until the surface begins to bubble.

In a large bowl, combine the remaining ⅔ cup warm milk, half of the melted butter, salt, onion powder, and sugar. Beat with a balloon whip until the sugar is dissolved. Then add the beaten eggs and the bubbly yeast.

Using an electric mixer, add the flour, ¼ cup at a time, and beat at high speed for about 5 minutes. When the dough gets too stiff to beat, stir in the rest of the flour and the onion flakes with a large spoon, making a soft and pliable dough. Turn out onto a floured surface and knead with your hands for 4–5 minutes, until the dough is smooth and satiny.

Place the dough in a large buttered bowl, turning the dough ball to coat all surfaces with butter. Cover the dough with a large plate and let it rise in a warm place until it doubles in size, about an hour.

Punch down the dough and, with a rolling pin, roll it out onto a floured surface to a ½-inch thickness. Cut into rounds with a 3-inch cookie cutter or small drinking glass you continually dip in flour.

Brush each round with melted butter (using a total of 4 tablespoons) and then fold the rounds in half to make half-moon shapes, pinching the edges together. Place rolls in a greased baking pan, put it back in the oven (use the boiling water in oven trick), cover with a dry cloth towel, and let rise until the dough doubles again.

Heat barbecue grill (or oven) to 350°F for grilling over indirect heat.

Bake the onion rolls in a covered barbecue for 20–25 minutes over indirect heat, rotating the pan 180°F once after 12 minutes. Remove when they're golden brown on top.

Before serving, brush the rolls with the remaining (4 tablespoons) melted butter.

SERVES 8-10
(24 ROLLS)

350°F
indirect grilling

1 cup whole milk

2 packets active dry yeast

16 tablespoons (2 sticks) butter, melted

¼ teaspoon salt

¼ teaspoon onion powder

¼ cup granulated sugar

¼ cup dried onion flakes

2 eggs, beaten

4½–5 cups all-purpose unbleached flour

Savory Seasonal Skillet Stuffing

SERVES 6-8

> 350°F
> indirect grilling

8 tablespoons (1 stick) butter

3 tablespoons olive oil

4 cups thinly sliced onions

½ cup dry vermouth

1 tablespoon freshly minced garlic

8 cups French bread cut into chunks

2 cups grated Emmenthaler or Swiss cheese

3 eggs

2 cups half-and-half

Sea salt

Freshly ground black pepper

If you prefer to cook your turkey without stuffing, this is a perfect recipe for a delicious savory side dish. This skillet dish is equally wonderful with roast beef and ham.

Heat barbecue grill (or oven) to 350°F for grilling over indirect heat.

On a side burner, over medium heat, melt 4 tablespoons butter with 2 tablespoons of the olive oil in a nonstick skillet. Add the onions, cover, and sauté over low heat for 12–15 minutes, until onions are translucent and just beginning to brown.

Turn the heat to medium-high and, while stirring constantly, cook until the onions caramelize and turn brown. Pour in the vermouth and boil until all the liquid evaporates. Add the garlic.

Prepare an 11- or 12-inch cast-iron skillet by brushing the sides and bottom thoroughly with the remaining olive oil.

In a large bowl, mix the bread chunks and onions together, stir well, and spoon the mixture into the oiled skillet. Melt the remaining butter and pour over the bread-onion mixture. Sprinkle with the cheese.

Beat the eggs slightly, add the half-and-half, and pour the mixture evenly over the bread and cheese. Lightly season with salt and pepper. Using a large spoon, stir to make sure the liquid is infused into the bread mix.

Bake, covered, for 30–40 minutes in the barbecue grill over indirect heat until puffed and golden. Place a water pan under the skillet if you prefer a moist stuffing. Remove from heat, let cool for 5 minutes, then serve in large triangular wedges.

Yorkshire Pudding — England's Culinary Gift to the World

*F*irst and foremost, it isn't a pudding. Nope. Not even close.

Yorkshire pudding is actually first cousin to a popover. If you're not familiar with that genre, I would describe it as sort of a muffin without any insides. It's an airy bit of tasty crust with no middle. A puff pastry, if you will, without anything but hot air in the puff.

The pudding was invented by poor folks way back in the early days of jolly old England as a way of stretching meals. When meat, like roast beef, was very expensive and mainly served in rich folks' kitchens, a plateful of Yorkshire pudding before the main meal would fill the stomach, leaving less room, or need, for that pricey protein.

The first published mention of this dish was in The Whole Duty of a Woman, *a quaintly and blatantly sexist, methinks, cookbook written around 1737. With that title, I shudder to think of how the book would sell these days.*

First called "dripping pudding," a flour-water-egg batter was placed in a shallow pan under a joint or roast of meat happily cooking on a spit over a fire. The batter puffed up and soaked up all those yummy meat juices and cascades of fat dripping from the cooking meat. Since fat was a good thing then, and people didn't have the fat-loaded diets of the twenty-first century, the tasty soaked hunks of pastry were an important part of their diet. Today, not so much.

Yorkshire pudding is usually cooked two different ways, as a large single pudding baked in a shallow dish or as individual "puds" in a muffin tin. There's actually an official Yorkshire pudding pan as well, with flatter and shallower cups for the batter. But the muffin tin is good enough for most of us, purists aside.

Even today some of those stodgy old sots insist on serving the dish BEFORE the meal, ladled with gravy. Younds! The thought of filling up with pastry and gravy before the first bite of drippingly moist roast beef fills me with angst.

"Yorkshires," as local English call the savory pastries, can also accompany roast chicken, turkey, pork, lamb, or just about any other meat roast or joint. But those stodgy oldsters and I agree that there is no more perfect accompaniment to a perfectly cooked roast of beef than the puddings. Accompaniment yes, but NOT as an appetizer!

Those in the pudding-know say that the pastries should be light, airy, and crisply browned on the outside. A batter made from flour, eggs, water, milk, and salt — some of the cheapest food ingredients then and now — are simply baked in the drippings from a roast. Easy enough.

Some chefs, though, want to add spices, herbs, and other stuff to the batter, but most folks, especially in the north of England, say you can't beat the original. Actually you have to beat it, and beat it well, so the batter gets frothy and fluffy and rises to the occasion.

And for the King's sake, don't use self-rising flour or add baking powder; they cause the puddings to bake up soggy, spongelike, and flat.

Okay, we've whet your appetite enough; now for some cooking tips.

As I said above, you can cook one big ol' "pud" in a large roasting pan or Pyrex dish or cast-iron skillet. Or you can make up individual ones. Up to you. I think the smaller puddings are better, as you don't need to hack up a large pudding at the table trying to cut them into equal sizes.

First start out the barbecue, or oven, heated to 350°F to cook the meat. Since you'll be cooking the roast at a much lower degree than the puddings, you need some kitchen know-how to accomplish this without a second barbecue or oven. You're saved by the fact that the roast should be removed from the oven at 135°F (for medium-rare).

The meat should be covered with foil and set aside to "rest" for 20–30 minutes. Be aware that the internal temperature will continue to rise the 10° or so needed to reach the perfect serving temperature of 145°F. Carefully pour the drippings into a small bowl or large measuring cup.

Stoke up the fires as it were; add some more charcoal, turn up the gas, or crank the oven dial up to 425°F.

Pour a tablespoonful of drippings, or, if you don't have drippings, drop a piece of lard the size of a thumb tip, into each muffin cup. If you're doing one large pudding, add 5–6 tablespoons of drippings to the pan and swirl it around.

Place the pan in the oven immediately, while it's heating up to 425°F. When it reaches that temperature (the fat should be smoking), remove the very hot muffin pan with a potholder or barbecue glove and place it on a heatproof counter, barbecue shelf, or stovetop.

Since you've made the batter already and have had it chilling in the refrigerator for at least 30 minutes, you can then begin to pour the batter into each cup. Fill each one a third full, then immediately put the pan into the hottest part of the barbecue or oven, closing the lid.

Puddings will be done in 20–25 minutes, just in time for the roast and everything else that you're serving. One large pudding will take about 30–40 minutes, yet another reason to do the individual ones.

A muffin pan of Yorkshire puddings hot from the oven should have nicely risen puddings that are golden brown and crisp outside, with a soft middle.

Oh yeah, a warning: When they come out of the oven, they're nicely puffed up, rising 2–3 inches above the pan, but they deflate quickly. Don't worry, that's what they should do. They're getting ready to soak up some gravy and meat juices on your plate. Stop, I'm drooling already.

So that's it folks, the history of the diminutive, ubiquitous, UK-style Yorkshire pudding. Simple ingredients, simply cooked, that produce the perfect accent to that perfect prime rib roast beef you've mortgaged your house to buy.

There almost certainly will be no leftovers.

❄

Mrs. Petersen's Yorkshire Pudding

425–450°F
direct grilling

4 large eggs, beaten

¾ teaspoon salt

1½ cups sifted all-purpose
  unbleached flour

1 cup whole milk

1 cup water

Hot grease/drippings from
  just-cooked roast

Mrs. *Petersen is my daughter, Kara, and this is one of her favorite dishes. I make it for almost all of our holiday dinners and now she's the expert, making it for her family, much to their delight. She likes to add a pinch of rosemary, oregano, and thyme to the batter.*

Heat barbecue grill (or oven) to 425–450°F° for direct heating.

In a large bowl, add the eggs and salt to a mound of sifted flour. Beat with a wooden spoon until elastic. Using a hand-mixer, stir the mixture, gradually adding the milk, until batter is smooth. Then beat in the water. Set aside. (In fact, some people say the best "puddings" come from batter that is refrigerated, covered, overnight, and then used cold.)

When your roast (beef, pork, or even chicken and turkey) is done, remove the meat from the barbecue. Take the roast (or fowl) out of the pan you've cooked it in and let it rest, covered in aluminum foil, so the juices return to the center of the meat, 20–30 minutes.

Meanwhile, using a silicone heat-resistant brush, coat the sides of each cup of a muffin pan (all the way to the top) with 1 tablespoon of the hot drippings from the roasting pan. Place the muffin pan in the barbecue and heat the drippings to just smoking. While this is happening, stir the batter with a hand-mixer for 1 minute.

Using a barbecue glove or oven potholders, transfer the muffin pan to a heatproof surface and quickly pour the batter a third of the way up the sides of each muffin cup.

Immediately move the pan back into the center of the barbecue, close the lid, and cook for 25–30 minutes until the puddings are crispy brown outside and soft and moist inside. The batter will have risen up and over the sides of the cups like large popovers.

A tip from Chef Lawrence Keogh, of Roast, one of London's most incredible restaurants, where I had the best roast beef and Yorkshire pudding of my life: "Halfway through the cooking, at about 14 to 15 minutes, you should carefully turn the pan on its side and use a knife or fork to flip each pudding over so that the bottom of each pudding gets crisp like the top."

Immediately serve each person one or two of the golden puddings with slices of rare or medium-rare roast beef.

Rustic Garlic-Mashed Potatoes

SERVES 6-8

350°F
direct grilling
wood chips

2 heads garlic, split halfway
from top to bottom

3 tablespoons olive oil

2 pounds white potatoes,
scrubbed and cut into
¼-inch slices

8 tablespoons (1 stick)
butter, very soft

Heavy cream

Flaked sea salt

Freshly ground black pepper

Paprika or freshly minced
parsley, for garnish

Pat of butter for garnish

*"R*ustic," *when used with mashed potatoes, usually means that you leave the skins on the potatoes when cooking and that you shouldn't mash the potatoes into a smooth consistency. Leave some small "chunks" of potato, skins, and garlic for character.*

Soak a handful of wood chips (hickory, oak, or fruitwood) in water for at least ½ hour before you are ready to grill.

Heat barbecue grill (or oven) to 350°F for grilling over direct heat.

Place the garlic halves, cut-side up, in a cast-iron skillet and drizzle with 2 tablespoons of the olive oil.

Put a handful of presoaked wood chips in a 12-inch square of aluminum foil. Seal the foil over the wood like an envelope, poke 2–3 holes in the top (do not go through the bottom), and place directly on the coals or gas flames in the grill. This will give a nice smoky flavor to the garlic.

Put the skillet with the garlic in the covered grill and cook for 30–35 minutes, or until the cloves are tender and the tops of the garlic halves have lightly browned. Remove the skillet, put the cloves in a small bowl, and let them cool.

Place the unpeeled potatoes in a pot of salted water and bring to a full boil, then reduce the heat to a simmer and cook the potatoes until just fork-tender, about 12–15 minutes. Remove the pan from the heat and drain thoroughly.

While the potatoes are cooking, squeeze the garlic cloves from the papery heads onto a plate. Using a garlic press, crush them into a small bowl and stir with a small whisk or fork until you have a smooth mash. Add the remaining tablespoon of olive oil and stir.

Once the potatoes are drained and dry, return them to the pot, add the garlic mash and the butter, and whip with a handheld mixer. Add enough cream, ¼ cup at a time, until the mashed potatoes hold nice peaks. There will be lumps — remember that's the "rustic" part. Season with the salt and pepper.

Scoop into a large serving bowl and place a nice pat of butter on top. Sprinkle with freshly minced parsley or lightly dust with paprika.

White and Gold Potato Patties

For a different twist on this recipe, add ½ cup of shredded or julienned apples or slivered green onions (about 3 inches long, including the white part). Or maybe add both. If you do so, add another egg.

❅

Heat barbecue grill (or oven) to 450°F for grilling over direct heat.

In a large mixing bowl, combine the mashed white and sweet potatoes, carrots, onion, eggs, flour, salt and pepper, mayonnaise, and crushed crackers. Mix well. Form the mixture into small (2- to 3-inch diameter) patties with your hands, which you've rubbed with flour.

Place a skillet or Dutch oven on the grill, or use the flat griddle that came with the barbecue. Add 2 tablespoons of bacon fat-olive oil mixture. Cook 5 or 6 patties at a time, frying to a deep, golden brown on each side. Remove to a heated platter, add more oil to pan, and grill remaining patties.

Serve warm, lightly sprinkled with garlic salt.

**SERVES 6-8
(MAKES 14-16 PATTIES)**

> 450°F
> direct grilling

2 cups mashed white or Yukon gold potatoes

1 cup mashed sweet potatoes

½ cup diced carrots, cooked until very soft

¾ cup thinly sliced onion

2 eggs, beaten

6 tablespoons all-purpose flour

Salt and freshly ground black pepper

½ cup olive oil mayonnaise

1 cup finely crushed Ritz crackers (or other favorite, not Saltines)

¼ cup melted bacon fat mixed with ¼ cup extra-virgin olive oil

Garlic salt

Orange and White Au Gratins

400°F
indirect grilling

¼ cup grated cheddar cheese

¼ cup crumbled blue cheese

3½ tablespoons extra-virgin olive oil

2 pounds Yukon gold potatoes

1 pound sweet potatoes

3 tablespoons butter, melted

½ teaspoon garlic salt

½ teaspoon freshly ground black pepper

1 cup nonfat milk

¼ cup heavy cream

¾ cup Ritz cracker crumbs (about 1 sleeve crushed)

This cheesy treatment is a good way to mix colors, flavors, and textures of starchy vegetables. If the cheddar and blue cheeses are too strong, substitute Gouda and Emmenthaler (Swiss) in the same amounts. Try the new Roasted Vegetable variety of the crackers; they add a wonderful, almost herbal taste.

Heat barbecue grill (or oven) to 400°F for grilling over indirect heat.

In a small bowl, mix the cheddar and blue cheeses and stir. Set aside.

Prepare a medium-size ovenproof baking dish (1.5- to 2-quart) by spraying the insides with a nonstick cooking spray. Add 1 tablespoon olive oil to the dish and swirl to coat the bottom.

Peel and slice all the potatoes into ¼-inch-thick slices. Cover the bottom of the oiled baking dish with a layer of Yukon gold potato slices, then follow with a layer of sweet potato slices. Sprinkle with half of the cheese. Pour 1 tablespoon melted butter and 1 tablespoon olive oil over the potatoes, then season with half of the garlic salt and pepper.

Repeat the sequence with the remaining Yukon gold and sweet potatoes, the second tablespoon of melted butter, a tablespoon of olive oil, and the remaining garlic salt and pepper. Then sprinkle on the remaining cheese.

Heat the milk and cream in a small saucepan over medium heat until boiling, then immediately pour it over the potatoes. Cover the top with the crushed crackers. Drizzle remaining 1 tablespoon of butter and the remaining ½ tablespoon of olive oil over the top.

Bake on the unheated side of the covered barbecue for 40–45 minutes until browned and bubbling. Let the potatoes rest for 5 minutes before serving.

Hawaiian Sweet Potatoes

If you're not a pineapple fan, you can substitute chopped mango, fresh peaches, or rehydrated or fresh apricots instead of the prickly Hawaiian fruit, and if you're macadamia impaired, use chopped pecans or walnuts.

Heat barbecue grill (or oven) to 350°F for grilling over direct heat.

In a large bowl, mix the potatoes, pineapple, brown sugar, salt, eggs, melted butter, cream, and vanilla. Stir to blend. Pour into greased baking dish or Dutch oven.

Mix all the topping ingredients together in a small bowl and sprinkle over the top of the casserole.

Place casserole into the covered barbecue and cook for 30–35 minutes. When casserole is brown on top and bubbling, it's ready.

SERVES 6-8

> 350°F
> direct grilling

3 cups mashed sweet potatoes (fresh or canned)

½ cup crushed pineapple

¾ cup brown sugar

½ teaspoon salt

2 eggs

4 tablespoons (½ stick) butter, melted

½ cup cream or half-and-half

1 teaspoon vanilla extract (or coconut rum)

Topping:

1 cup brown sugar

1 cup chopped macadamia nuts

⅓ cup flour

4 tablespoons (½ stick) butter, melted

Parmigiano-Reggiano-Shallot Risotto

SERVES 4-6

> 350°F
> indirect grilling

2 tablespoons butter

4 cups thinly sliced crimini mushrooms

¼ teaspoon garlic salt

¼ teaspoon freshly ground black pepper

½ cup finely chopped shallots

2 teaspoons minced fresh chives

½ teaspoon dried oregano

½ teaspoon dried thyme

2 cups short-grain white rice

1½ cups dry white wine

2½ cups vegetable stock

½ cup freshly grated Parmigiano-Reggiano cheese

⅓ cup coarsely chopped fresh parsley

Paprika for garnish

Parmigiano-Reggiano is perhaps the finest cheese on earth and cannot be substituted for — well it can, but don't. Parmesan is actually the French word for this Italian family of cheeses. Parmigiano-Reggiano is more expensive than generic Parmesan cheeses, but the rich texture and flavor make it well worth the extra cost. My friends and family are worth it, aren't yours?

Heat barbecue grill (or oven) to 350°F for grilling over indirect heat.

In a large, deep cast-iron skillet or Dutch oven on a barbecue side burner or stovetop, melt the butter over medium-high heat, then add the mushrooms, garlic salt, pepper, shallots, chives, oregano, and thyme. Cook until the mushrooms are golden and shallots are tender, about 5–7 minutes.

Add the rice and stir until well coated, then add the wine and stock and bring to a full boil.

Transfer the skillet or Dutch oven to the preheated barbecue grill and cook over indirect heat, with the lid closed, until all of the liquid has been absorbed and the rice is tender but firm in the center, about 25–30 minutes. Do not stir while it's cooking.

Remove the skillet from the barbecue, stir in the Parmesan cheese and parsley, and garnish with a sprinkling of paprika.

Creamed Peas with Mint

There are more than 30 varieties of mint, an herb that dates back to the Romans and Greeks. They used it in religious ceremonies, as an herb, in perfume, in their baths, and even, powdered, to brush their teeth and freshen their breath. Mmmmmmm — a really minty mouthwash. The variety commonly sold in the supermarket, and used here, is spearmint.

Heat barbecue grill (or oven) to 350° F for grilling over direct heat.

In a medium bowl, dissolve cornstarch in heavy cream, then add sour cream and sugar, and stir to mix. Set aside.

In a cast-iron skillet on the grill or side burner, sauté the onions in butter until soft and barely browned, 10–12 minutes. Add the mint, peas, wine, and water. When the peas come to a boil, stir in the cream mixture. Heat on the barbecue for an additional 2 minutes, stirring constantly.

Remove the skillet from the grill, pour the creamed peas into a bowl, and keep warm until ready to serve. Garnish with a sprinkle of fresh or dried mint.

SERVES 4-6

350°F
direct grilling

1 tablespoon cornstarch

3 tablespoons heavy cream

¼ cup sour cream

½ teaspoon sugar

2 cups pearl onions (fresh, jarred and rinsed, or frozen and thawed)

2 tablespoons butter

3 tablespoons chopped fresh mint leaves (or 1½ tablespoons dried mint), plus a little extra for garnish

1 pound fresh or frozen (thawed) peas

½ cup white wine

½ cup water

Granny Kate's Korn Puddin'

> 350°F
> indirect grilling
> water pan

1 (8½-ounce) box corn muffin mix (Jiffy recommended)

1 (16-ounce) can whole kernel corn with juice

1 (16-ounce) can creamed corn

1 can (4-ounce) mild chopped green chili peppers

1 small onion, minced

¾ cup shredded cheddar cheese

8 tablespoons (1 stick) melted butter or margarine

1 cup sour cream

2 eggs

This is my family's favorite holiday side dish, and my wife Kate loves it when our four grandchildren call her "Granny." This recipe was passed down to her from her father, who was the cook in her family. Well, her Mom did cook up ham occasionally.

Heat barbecue grill (or oven) to 350°F for indirect heating, with water pan under unheated side.

In a large bowl, mix together all the ingredients, and stir until blended.

Pour into a buttered roasting pan or skillet sprayed with nonstick butter-flavored spray.

Bake, with grill lid closed, on the unheated side of the grill, over the water pan, for 45–50 minutes or until the top is lightly browned.

Honey-Butter Brussels Sprouts

SERVES 4-6

350°F
direct grilling

*W*hen choosing Brussels sprouts, pick those that are bright green, small, firm, and compact, with no blemished leaves. They will keep in the refrigerator for up to 5 days in "green" or perforated plastic bags. Cut an "X" into the bottom of each sprout so the core cooks at the same rate as the leaves.

Heat barbecue grill (or oven) to 350°F for grilling over direct heat.

In a large cast-iron skillet, cook bacon and onions until bacon is cooked but not crisp, about 5 minutes. With a slotted spoon, remove bacon and onions, leaving remaining bacon fat, and set aside.

Arrange the Brussels sprouts cut-side down in the skillet. Sprinkle with salt and pepper, then pour the honey, melted butter, and white wine over the sprouts. Close grill cover and cook until the sprouts are fork-tender, about 8 minutes.

Stir the bacon and onions into the skillet and heat for an additional 3–4 minutes.

Serve in a warmed bowl.

4 strips bacon, cut into
  1-inch pieces

¼ cup chopped onions

1½ pounds fresh Brussels
  sprouts, cut in half lengthwise

¼ teaspoon salt

Freshly ground black pepper

¼ cup honey

¼ cup melted butter

4 tablespoons white wine

Skillet-Grilled Root Vegetables

SERVES 6-8

350°F
direct grilling

1 cup ¼-inch-thick sliced carrots

1 cup ½-inch cubes peeled acorn squash

1 cup ½-inch cubes peeled butternut squash

1 cup ¼-inch cubes peeled turnips

1 cup ¼-inch cubes peeled parsnips

8 tablespoons (1 stick) butter, melted

½ cup pure maple syrup

2 garlic cloves, minced

1½ tablespoons chopped fresh rosemary

1 teaspoon dried thyme

1 teaspoon dried savory

1 teaspoon salt

½ teaspoon freshly ground black pepper

4 tablespoons (½ stick) melted butter

1 cup Panko breadcrumbs

If you haven't "seasoned" your cast-iron skillet or Dutch oven recently, you should do so once a year or so. Merely coat the bottom and inside of the pan with oil or shortening, wipe out most of it, then bake upside down in a 400–500°F oven or barbecue for 1 hour. Cool, then repeat twice more. This will season the skillet for a year.

Cook sliced carrots in 2 cups water until tender; drain and set aside.

Heat barbecue grill (or oven) to 350°F for grilling over direct heat.

Butter or spray with olive-oil spray a cast-iron Dutch oven or large skillet; set aside.

Combine the cooked carrots, acorn and butternut squash, turnips, and parsnips in the prepared Dutch oven or skillet.

Pour the melted butter into a small bowl, then add the maple syrup, garlic, rosemary, thyme, savory, salt, and pepper. Stir to mix well. Pour over the root vegetables and gently stir to coat them.

Cover the vegetables tightly with a lid or aluminum foil, and bake for 35–40 minutes on the covered grill. Remove from grill. Pour the melted butter over the breadcrumbs and immediately stir to coat. Sprinkle over the root vegetables and return Dutch oven to grill with lid closed, until all the vegetables are tender, and the crumbs are starting to brown, about 20 minutes longer.

SixNine Pecan Pie

borrowed a recipe from Kevin Belton, who owns Lil' Dizzy's Café in New Orleans, and made a few changes with his approval. The name comes from the fact he's 6'9" tall, was once a defensive tackle for the San Diego Chargers, and uses "sixnine" as his e-mail address. I don't know how well he tackled, but man, oh man, can he ever cook!

Heat barbecue grill (or oven) to 325°F for grilling over indirect heat.

In a medium bowl, combine the melted butter, brown sugar, corn syrup, molasses, cinnamon, nutmeg, cloves, eggs, Grand Marnier, and cream.

Place the 12 reserved pecan halves in a small bowl and gently mix with the warm honey; set aside.

Fold the remaining pecans into the butter-sugar-egg mixture; then spoon into the prepared pie shell. Place pie pan on a baking sheet or a double thickness of heavy-duty aluminum foil, and decorate the top of the pie with the reserved honey-covered pecan halves.

Bake on the indirect heat side of the barbecue until filling is set, 35–45 minutes. Check for doneness by inserting a toothpick into the center of the pie; when it comes out clean, pie is done.

Cool to room temperature before serving with freshly whipped cream.

SERVES 6-8

325°F
indirect grilling

6 tablespoons unsalted butter, melted

1 ¼ cups packed dark brown sugar

½ cup corn syrup

½ cup molasses

⅛ teaspoon ground cinnamon

¼ teaspoon ground nutmeg

Pinch of ground cloves

4 large eggs, lightly beaten

2 teaspoons Grand Marnier

¼ cup light or heavy cream

1 ½ cups whole pecans (reserve 12 of the best for garnish)

2 tablespoons warm honey

1 9-inch prebaked pie shell

Freshly whipped cream

Tricia's Barbecue Bread Pudding

SERVES 6-8

350°F
indirect grilling

12 (½-inch-thick) slices of French bread

6 large egg whites

2 egg yolks

1¼ cups brown sugar

1½ teaspoons dark rum

1¼ teaspoons ground cinnamon

½ teaspoon grated lemon zest

2 tablespoons unsalted butter, melted

1 cup skim milk

1 cup cream or half-and-half

½ cup milk chocolate chips

½ cup golden raisins

Maple syrup (the real thing, please!)

Freshly whipped cream

Since my daughter Tricia LOVES sweets, I developed this recipe in her honor. This is sweet to be sure with brown sugar, chocolate chips, raisins, and maple syrup, but as a special treat it will bring you applause.

Heat barbecue grill (or oven) to 350° F for grilling over indirect heat.

Grill the bread slices directly over medium heat until toasted and grill marks appear, about 2 minutes, turning once halfway through the grilling time. Cut the bread into cubes (approximately 5 cups) and set aside.

In a large bowl, beat the egg whites until they are frothy. Add the egg yolks, brown sugar, rum, cinnamon, lemon zest, and melted butter. Stir vigorously until the mixture is well blended. Add the milk and cream, then stir in the chocolate chips and raisins. Add the toasted bread cubes and toss until mixed well. Let the mixture rest for about 45 minutes, patting the bread down into the liquid occasionally.

Butter a 5x9-inch loaf pan or spray with nonstick spray. Pour in the bread-egg mixture. Place the pan on the unheated side of the barbecue grill, cover grill, and bake for 50–60 minutes or until the top of the dessert is well-browned and puffed up.

Slice, drizzle with real maple syrup, and serve warm with a generous dollop of freshly whipped cream. (If you use a canned whipped cream, I'll never speak to you again).

Hausfrau's German Chocolate Soufflé

On several trips to Germany, I've loved the real homemade German Chocolate Cake served to me in a number of homes I visited. I wanted to see how I could make a soufflé that tasted like a slice of this wonderful cake. I think this recipe works pretty well. "Hausfrau" in German means "housewife."

Heat barbecue grill (or oven) to 375°F for grilling over indirect heat.

Generously butter and sugar the sides and bottom of a 4- to 6-serving, straight-sided soufflé dish. Tap out the excess sugar.

Using butcher's twine, tie a triple-thick collar of aluminum foil that reaches from the bottom of the dish to 3 inches above the top. Butter and sugar the inside of the foil. Spread the jar of cherry preserves over the bottom of the buttered and sugared soufflé dish. Sprinkle with the kirsch.

Using a balloon whisk or an electric mixer, beat the egg whites until they form stiff peaks. Add cream of tartar as you begin whipping.

In a medium saucepan over low heat, beat the yolks, and then add cocoa, coconut, and confectioners' sugar little by little, until it is well mixed.

Very gently fold the whites into 1 cup of the egg yolk base so as not to break up the bubbles in the egg whites. Then gently fold this mixture into the remaining yolk base. When fully combined, gently spoon the soufflé mixture over the cherry preserves.

Bake in the covered barbecue over indirect heat for 24–26 minutes, until the soufflé rises and turns brown on top, but is still jiggly in the middle. Carefully remove the dish from the barbecue and serve immediately.

SERVES 4-6

375°F
indirect grilling
twine

8 tablespoons (1 stick) butter, softened

Granulated sugar (for coating soufflé dish)

1 (12-ounce) jar of cherry preserves (do not use jam)

2 tablespoons kirsch liqueur (optional)

5 eggs, separated, at room temperature

1 teaspoon cream of tartar

3 tablespoons unsweetened cocoa powder

½ cup unsweetened flaked coconut

4 tablespoons confectioners' sugar

Eggnog Popovers

450°F

indirect grilling

---

1 cup all-purpose flour

2 tablespoons instant eggnog
powder

½ teaspoon ground nutmeg

¼ teaspoon ground cinnamon

½ teaspoon salt

1 tablespoon unsalted
butter, melted

3 large eggs

1 cup whole milk

½ teaspoon rum extract
(or real rum)

4 tablespoons (½ stick)
melted butter for popover
or muffin pan

Confectioner's sugar for
dusting

Look for eggnog powder in health food stores, the health foods section of your supermarket, or online. I use Barry Farm Foods (www.barryfarm.com/flavorings.htm), which adds a nice egg-noggy flavor with no effort.

Heat barbecue grill (or oven) to 450°F for grilling over indirect heat.

In a large bowl, mix together the flour, eggnog powder, nutmeg, cinnamon, and salt.

In a separate small bowl, whisk together the melted butter, eggs, milk, and rum extract.

Stir the milk mixture into the flour mixture, stirring just until the batter is mixed, being careful not to overbeat the batter.

In the preheated barbecue or oven, heat a muffin pan for 5 minutes, or until it is very hot. Brush each of the cups with melted butter, and fill them half-full with the batter. Bake the popovers on the hot side of the covered barbecue for 20 minutes, then move them to indirect heat for an additional 20 minutes more, or until they are golden brown and crisp.

Dust with confectioner's sugar and serve immediately.

Mrs. Browne's Butter Tarts

There's a reason most of the recipes in this chapter are named for various members of my family — we all love desserts! But this recipe is approximately 100 years old, passed to my mother from her mother, and then passed on to my wife, two daughters, and two sons. It's a very Canadian dessert, found in bakeries everywhere north of the border but seldom in this country. No matter, we make our own.

✳

Heat barbecue grill (or oven) to 350°F for grilling over indirect heat.

Plump the raisins and currants in boiling water for 5 minutes, then drain well on paper toweling in the bottom of a colander.

Beat the eggs well. Add the brown sugar, syrup, and melted butter and beat again. Add the raisins, currants, vinegar, salt, and vanilla extract. Stir vigorously.

Roll the prepared pie crust dough to ⅛-inch thickness. Cut out 3- to 3½-inch-diameter circles of the dough. Spray nonstick butter-flavored spray into tart tins or muffin pans, then place the dough rounds into the pans, filling all the way up to the rim.

Fill the shells two-thirds full with the sugar-raisin mixture. Bake over indirect heat, with grill lid down, for about 20 minutes, until the pastry is light brown and the filling is bubbling.

Let tarts rest for at least 15 minutes before eating, as the filling is extremely hot and can burn your mouth.

SERVES 4-6
(MAKES 24 TARTS)

350°F
indirect grilling

- 1 cup raisins
- ½ cup currants
- 2 large eggs
- 1½ cups dark brown sugar
- ½ cup corn syrup (or pure maple syrup)
- 3 tablespoons butter, melted
- 2 teaspoons white vinegar
- Pinch of salt
- ½ teaspoon vanilla extract
- One batch of prepared pie crust dough

Index